Praise for **10,000 MILES WITH MY DEAD FATHER'S ASHES**

"With asides spanning from his pot-smoking, pill-popping teenage years to his later adult failures as an average American man, this…hoot of a memoir rings with themes that will appeal to many readers coming-of-age in the 1970s and '80s. A candid and humorous tale."

—*Kirkus Reviews*

"Riveting, funny, emotional. I laughed out loud and cried real tears."

—**Krista Vernoff**, executive producer of *Grey's Anatomy*,
Shameless, and *Charmed*

"Devin Galaudet writes that his dad 'wanted to lift off the lid to life for me and show me its flailing innards' and that's what Galaudet does, himself, in these pages—he lifts the lid off a complicated, volatile, father-son relationship and shows us all that is flailing and painful and hilarious and poignant within. Galaudet's journey with his father is deeply, engrossingly, unique, yet also has much to say about what it means to come of age as a man in America. A compelling and unforgettable read."

–**Gayle Brandeis**, author of *The Art of Misdiagnosis:
Surviving My Mother's Suicide*

"How do you write a travel book about a serious topic…while still keeping it fun and highly readable? I had no idea—until I came across *10,000 Miles*. This is a story that needs to be widely read."

—**Chris Guillebeau,** *New York Times* bestselling author of
The Art of Non-Conformity

"An achingly poignant odyssey consummately crafted and disguised as a personal family memoir."

—**Lon Milo DuQuette**, author of *My Life with the Spirits*

"[Devin's] writing is creatively intriguing, well crafted, with a very strong narrative voice."

—**Alma Villanueva**, author of *Song of the Golden Scorpion*

"Devin Galaudet captures the wrenching, often funny intricacies of grieving for a less than perfect father. Love and violence, abandonment and slapstick comedy commingle in this poignant and real story of how we come to terms with our parents in their varied and often complex manifestations."

—**Kate Maruyama**, author of *Harrowgate*

"Devin Galaudet has taken on one of the toughest subjects a writer…and a man…can attempt: coming to terms with his relationship to his father and summoning the courage for a final goodbye. Galaudet writes with a great eye for physical detail, compassion, intensity, and humor. *10,000 Miles with My Dead Father's Ashes* promises to be a guidebook for the rest of us who might undertake a similar emotional journey."

—**Kent Black**, editor in chief at *Palm Springs Life* magazine

"Galaudet writes with a voice that is vulnerable and even painful at times, but it's also always entertaining and downright funny. He's clearly an excellent storyteller and traveling around the world with him would undoubtedly be a blast! His writing is the next best thing."

—**Kenneth Shapiro**, editor in chief of *TravelAge West*

"Devin Galaudet tells his story of love and loss with humor and poignancy. This is a candid, moving work about a scared boy trying to find a way to be a grown man."

—**Telaina Eriksen**, 2010 and 2011 Pushcart Prize nominee

"Anyone who's scattered a parent's ashes knows it is a confusing mix of sadness and irony. Devin captures both perfectly."

—**Peter Hancoff**, writer, producer, troublemaker

"Truly moving, cohesive, and rich in wry cynicism, Devin's writing is taut and can teach us all something about the love a son has for his father,"

—**Kat Kambes**, writer

"In small details like finding parking, Galaudet reveals the inner landscape of losing a parent, interspersing dark humor to give the reader the space to breathe through the intimacy of grief. Galaudet's travel memoir shows us that no matter how far you travel the language of grief and compassion are the same."

—**Angela M. Brommel**, author of *Plutonium & Platinum Blonde*

10,000 MILES WITH MY DEAD FATHER'S ASHES

OR MI PADRE ES MUERTO EN LA BOLSA

A Vireo Book | Rare Bird Books
Los Angeles, Calif.

10,000 MILES WITH MY DEAD FATHER'S ASHES

OR MI PADRE ES MUERTO EN LA BOLSA

DEVIN GALAUDET

This is a Genuine Vireo Book

A Vireo Book | Rare Bird Books
453 South Spring Street, Suite 302
Los Angeles, CA 90013
rarebirdbooks.com

FIRST TRADE PAPERBACK ORIGINAL EDITION

Set in Minion
Printed in the United States

10 9 8 7 6 5 4 3 2 1

Publisher's Cataloging-in-Publication data
Names: Galaudet, Devin, author.
Title: 10,000 Miles with my Dead Father's Ashes : Or Mi Padre es Muerto
en la Bolsa / Devin Galaudet.
Description: First Trade Paperback Original Edition | A Vireo Book |
New York, NY; Los Angeles, CA: Rare Bird Books, 2018.
Identifiers: ISBN 9781947856165
Subjects: LCSH Galaudet, Devin. | Galaudet, Devin—Family. | Fathers and
sons—Biography. | Fathers—Death. | Spain—Description and Travel. |
BISAC BIOGRAPHY & AUTOBIOGRAPHY / Personal Memoirs |
BIOGRAPHY & AUTOBIOGRAPHY / Literary
Classification: LCC HQ755.85 .G41 2018 | DDC 306.76/620922—dc23

For Shea to understand your exceptional yet flawed family tree.

Chapter 1

I HATE TO BE the one to tell you this, but your dad's dead." She spit it out in one piece. I stood in my living room in my underwear and bare feet with the phone glued to my ear. The gardener was outside my window using one of those contraptions that made an incessant grinding noise, but there was no doubt as to what I heard. And I knew it was true even though I hadn't told her who I was.

"Is this Devin?" she'd asked.

And I'd responded, "Who's calling?"

Dad taught me early not to offer too much. Maybe it was a collection agency or someone I had knocked up, or one of fifty other things I did not want to deal with at the time. I still answered the phone this way, likely from some residual fear I clung to that the world was not a friendly place, even though my life had been content for ages. I suppose old habits die hard.

The sensation swarmed up my body. I launched into big, uncontrollable, heaving sobs that left me shaking. Every time I slowed down, the crying returned. My reaction surprised me, as I had decided that Dad was nothing more than a distant pile of unresolved resentments. His death had been long expected and perhaps overdue, at least in the land of intellect.

My emotional terrain, however, was another story.

The call came from a woman named Cathy, who described herself as Dad's wife of fifteen years. She confided that she was thirty years his junior and that he helped raise her two daughters. Dad had died of a heart attack two weeks prior, lying on his stomach with a cigarette in his hand in their trailer in St. George, Utah, while Cathy was at work. Nothing seemed wrong when she left him in front of the television.

He had told Cathy several times that when he died, there was to be no funeral. He had instructed that no one from his family should know about his death until after he had been cremated. His dying wish was that he be scattered off the coast of Cádiz, Spain—to return home while "Ave Maria" played. Really, he wanted to be sent into outer space on a rocket, but he knew that was not going to happen. Cathy sighed before and after speaking, her words spilling out in one long, struggling breath.

I shook my head and gulped for air between tears. Dad wanted to return home to Spain? He wasn't from Spain. He was French, German, and Irish—and to my knowledge, he had never even been out of the United States. As for "Ave Maria," he would not be caught dead in a church. And he'd been living in a trailer park in Utah? He was a city guy.

None of it made sense.

✳✳✳

THE VOICE ON MY phone machine had said, "Devin, it's your father. I am at the train station—come and get me." I hadn't heard from him in three years. Once again, he had managed to trick me into thinking he was dead, which was a relief. After fifteen years of disappearances and returns from the grave, I decided he was like Dracula, a charismatic leech who would need to have a stake shoved through his heart to get rid of him. Clearly he was not ready to go and made a point of bothering me every blue moon.

Another message followed. "Devin, it's your father. I am at 7-Eleven. Come and get me."

At 12:22 a.m. the phone rang, my aunt on my mother's side letting me know that Dad was waiting at a specific 7-Eleven about half a mile from my house.

She should go get him, I thought. I was sleeping. Pretending to be interested in seeing him would be a chore, and I was finished.

I got out of bed and dressed anyway.

I pulled around the corner and into the 7-Eleven parking lot. He stood there under the dim fluorescent lights wearing a purple "Go Utah Jazz" T-shirt and plaid shorts. His hair was much thinner than I recalled, and I shuddered at the mortality of my own fraying hairline. I had never known him to wear purple or short pants or to have thinning hair. He weighed seventy-five pounds less than I had ever seen him before and his skinny white legs glowed pale in the light. I barely recognized him. He had always had wide shoulders, big arms, and a gut for days. He was the guy that taught me to stick up for myself and fight well outside the Marquess of Queensbury. He was now a former tough guy, and that did not compute with what I understood of the world. A nearby homeless man looked like he planned to roll Dad.

Life had caught up with him. He was a geezer, some old guy that had replaced my father. The father I knew had a presence that did not require explanation. The shell before me was weak and used up, something ineffable beyond weight loss, which screamed, "I give up." In an odd way, I saw him in the same way I looked at a lost child. My heart sank. I slowly put the car in park. I needed time to think and to prepare to act as if nothing were wrong.

As I exited the car, I said, "So, what do you say, Slim?" Dad stood there with his hands in his pockets and a cigarette sticking out perpendicular to his face, which held no expression. I threw an arm around his neck and kissed him on his cheek. He smelled of menthol cigarettes and men's cologne from a discount drugstore. I hadn't noticed the oversized suitcases at his feet and the large brass elephant that sat on top of them when I drove up.

He did not look at me, somehow sensing my disappointment. "Help your father in your car," he said. He always liked referring to himself in the third person.

It was late and I was feeling increasingly nauseated.

As I unloaded the car at my place, Dad sat on the porch and lit up a cigarette. I threw some linens and an old wool blanket that smelled of cedar and mothballs on the couch before schlepping in his luggage with the elephant.

We talked as if nothing had changed, although it had. He had disappeared one too many times, and I was exhausted from it all. I had moved on with my life without him.

Without getting up from the couch, he reached over and grabbed the elephant by the trunk and handed it to me. "I want you to have this," he said. It was awkwardly shaped, with huge ears that fanned out, and its trunk curled in front of its tusked face. I felt its weight and coldness.

"What am I supposed to do with this?"

"What are you, weird? It's from Africa."

"It not from Africa," I said. "It's swap meet fodder."

To an outsider, this may have sounded harsh, but Dad smiled, the first smile I had seen since I picked him up.

"Well, maybe not the real Africa," he said. "Just take the damn thing, it weighs a ton. You should get it melted down and make something else out of it, like a gazelle." Then he laughed to himself.

We chatted about nothing important. I never asked questions like *Where have you been for the last few years? Do you own a telephone?* I had already asked them before, many times. He would answer only, "Your old man, he's like the wind," or some other bullshit fortune-cookie answer. I sat there with the elephant in my lap in the rocking chair across from him until he let out a snore. I watched him for a minute, debating. Was he as pathetic as I thought he was? Was he worthy of my compassion? He wanted something, probably money, which I would eventually give him.

I put the elephant down in the middle of the room. Then I went to sleep.

In the morning, he could have eased into it, but instead he got right to the point of his visit. "Your old man needs a car," he blurted with coffee-and-cigarette breath. He then began to describe my old car—the car I had just had towed away by a charity that fulfills wishes to dying children. It had been sitting in the driveway for months collecting a layer of gray dust. I had no money to get it fixed and couldn't justify keeping it around any longer.

I apologized with a tinge of undeserved guilt and told him I would buy him a great steak dinner, something with lots of butter, when I got home from work. I felt as though I had let him down, again. As if I had rejected him. I showed him how to use the remote, kissed him, and gave him a twenty and the spare key to the front door.

I came home that evening to find the front door wide open. His two suitcases were gone, as were half the groceries from my fridge. The sheets on the couch were rolled into a ball and he forgot to leave my key. Or a note. He forgot to take the brass elephant, which still sat in the middle of the room. Still, I was relieved.

He died within the year. Had I known it would be the last time I would see him, I would not have changed the locks.

✳✳✳

I HUNG UP THE phone with Cathy and stood with my hands on my hips, looking around my apartment for clues as to what I should do next, trying to slow my breath and catch hiccups. I attempted to see him in my mind as tall, handsome, and strong and hoped to have fond memories flood me. Nothing came except how I stole two of his Budweisers and a pack of Salems into the yard one Thanksgiving to become a man without him.

I held on to the news for an hour before calling my father's twin sister, Gloria, first. My voice shook, and I was unable to get words out. She said, "Don't tell me anything. I don't want to know nothing," and hung up the phone.

Everyone else—uncles, aunts, cousins—said how much they loved him. How much he had given them. The stories started with how loving he was and I listened to them until they were through, could almost feel the shrugs that punctuated their stories.

And then they'd ask, "Whatever happened to him?"

I did not have many answers.

✳✳✳

IMMEDIATELY AFTER DAD DIED, there was a lull in my confused feelings about him. Over the next several weeks, Cathy and I talked regularly. At the time, I had not been to St. George, Utah, his last earthly home, and had no relevant details about anything in his life. Cathy told me what she could.

She told me she was thirty years Dad's junior, which made her only a couple years older than I. She had two daughters that Dad had helped raise since the girls were small. She talked about Dad with love in her voice and explained they had moved many times before they ended up in a trailer park in St. George, Utah, a place I eventually saw as both beautiful and isolated. They fought and split up more than once, and they always came back together. She stayed with him through illness. "I had to stop letting him drive," she said. She had a habit of pausing between sentences, as if she had disappeared from the conversation. "You never knew when one of those things would hit," to the seizures Dad began to experience a few years prior to his death.

Her voice rose and fell with concern, frustration, and hope as she talked, clearly having drunk the Kool-Aid. She believed everything he had fed her, a quality I was certain Dad liked best. The most significant and disturbing example was his brown briefcase. He told her its contents held a secret that would take care of her for the rest of her life but instructed her not to open it until *after* he died.

She waited a full week before cracking it open. In the brief time I had gotten to know Cathy, I learned that she had a hard life filled with family instability, a lack of opportunity, and little money. She must have seen Dad as a charming, good-natured man, and—in theory—a long-term provider. At the time of Dad's death, she had been working for the local market collecting baskets in the parking lot. While honest work, I cannot imagine this being the life she had planned out with Dad. He played her like he did me and everyone else.

As she described the suitcase scenario, I pictured her fumbling with a butter knife against some cheap, snapping combination lock covered in gold spray paint and glued to an imitation leather briefcase binding, and her brow crinkling at the possibility of some escape from her grind. I doubt she seriously believed her finances would be transformed by Dad's secret treasure, but she probably expected some breathing room from, say, a life insurance policy—some space to let her mourn properly.

I felt myself dreaming along with her toward a happy conclusion, hoping she would tell me she found some sustaining stash, even though I knew the ending of the story long before she got there.

She took a deep breath and sighed. "Well, after the briefcase opened, there were a few scraps of paper with some numbers on them. You know, nothing really important. One of the numbers was yours."

***

IN 1972, ALL BOYS wore the same Sears Toughskin jeans and camel-colored work boots. All of them except me. Mom dressed me in a collection of costumes that would have rivaled any sixteenth-century French dandy or Russian tablecloth. I wore knickers, pantaloons, and ruffled shirts; nothing I owned blended with the social norms of the current century.

All I wanted was a football jersey with a number quarterbacks wore. Instead, my closet was filled with oversized brass buckles, shiny fabrics, and inconvenient snaps all reflecting the sun in a most attention-seeking way. My mother demanded that I wear them, and for a while I did, at least until everyone in second grade started to notice that I was not blending.

Mom had told me it was for my own good, that I needed to do what I was told. I crawled along the yellow tile floor in little white underpants as my mother's foot crashed down on my head again. I wanted to agree with her, but my body recoiled from her instinctually. I was seven years old and living with my parents in the worst apartment in a good Jewish neighborhood in Los Angeles.

Dad remained oblivious to what I wore. He left at dawn and was either asleep or holed up in his room, lying on his belly watching the TV; or I barricaded myself in my room to isolate myself.

On one particular morning, I decided to never wear those clothes again.

Perhaps that was a mistake.

Control through force was normal for Mom. Whatever she dished out to me paled in comparison to the ruthless abuse she received from her parents. My grandparents came from Mother Russia or Poland or Ukraine, the boundaries moving with each passing military conflict. My grandfather picked potatoes in the fields when he was five, and when he was hungry he ate grass. My grandmother had scars on her back where the rats would bite her when she slept. They were each five feet two inches of surly, old-world logic. They didn't allow gifts or birthday presents and made Mom a punching bag often.

Years later, Mom had me.

Her left foot found my rib cage as I tried to wedge myself behind the bathroom sink. The oxygen ran from my lungs. I had become accustomed to this. Mom bent over and grabbed at my feet to pull me from under the sink. I tried to catch my breath. I thought, *Why was I fighting to get dressed?* I was ready to give in, forget the pledge I made to myself, and get dressed in anything she wanted.

Then the memory of my maroon-colored cap appeared.

They had tossed my maroon-colored cap high above my head, from one kid to another. "Give me back my cap," I said. One second grader who was missing his front teeth put the cap behind his back as I lunged for it before flinging it to another kid.

"Don't let it hit the ground," I said. "Do you know how much it costs to clean crushed velvet? My mother will kill me." They never listened, unless it was to repeat what I had just said in some awful impersonation.

My mother will kill me. My mother will kill me.

Was my voice really that high pitched?

After the cap had hit the ground a few times, I stopped chasing it. I could feel the emotions build in my throat. My face ran hot and red. My tight matching velvet pants and swashbuckling boots made me slow. I felt helpless and humiliated. In 1970s public school, turning red in the face was okay. Crying was not.

It was all I could do not to fall apart; I did not want to give them the satisfaction. I could not chase the cap and hold it together at the same time. I wrapped my arms around myself across my chest and tried to calm down, to appear under control while they danced around me. I wanted their mercy and that cap back. The game of Monkey in the Middle finally ended with the help of some dufus kid named Jimmy. While I stood there, he walked up to me and said, "Here, want your cap?" and extended the cap to me. When I reached for it, he threw it to the ground, closed his eyes, clenched his teeth, and threw a wild punch that hit me in the stomach.

I doubled over next to the crushed velvet cap.

The knees of my maroon pantaloons were slightly bloodied and frayed from the fall. On the way home, Mom was pissed, and she later waved the crumpled laundry receipt for that jackass cap in my face. I had let her down for not taking better care of my clothes. After all, if I brushed the velvet in different directions, it would change colors.

My feelings of remorse were soon removed by the pummeling I took over the tan-and-salmon macramé sweater vest. I was told that its appeal was that it was to be worn shirtless. The sweater's loose weave showed way too much skin, and the accompanying knot in my stomach was a clear omen of a playground throttling to come as I walked into class.

I never did count all the lumps I took that day or who was handing them out, but it wasn't until my mother complained about how hard it was to remove blood from yarn that I made a vow. Later that night, I swore I would never again go out dressed to provoke every pissed-off kid in the school. In the morning, I complained and cried and finally refused.

Mom had hold of my ankle and pulled me toward her. "Get dressed," she said. She was repeatedly slapping me across the head when I heard the front door slam shut. It was an unusual sound, as my father was generally nonexistent from dawn to dusk, but his heavy, lace-up boots coming down the hall were a welcome sound. My mother continued to hit me, unaware of his encroaching footsteps. He finally appeared in the doorway.

"What the fuck are you doing?" Dad said as he stopped at the bathroom door. His unexpected entrance startled Mom. Her face seemingly snapped into consciousness. She straightened herself up for confrontation.

"I said, what the fuck are you doing?"

Mom methodically picked up the pair of red corduroy knickers from the top of the sink. "He won't put these on," she said, and she confidently shook them in front of his face.

He looked at them for a moment. The electric hum from the light fixture took hold of the room as dread wilted me. It crossed my mind: *What if Dad thinks these pants are cool?* If he did, I knew I would look forward to many future playground beatings.

He took the knickers from her and unbunched them and inspected them for a moment. He then looked at me, tear-streaked, sitting between the bathtub and the sink, and then back at Mom. He said, "Well, fuck, I wouldn't fucking wear these things either. Were you hoping he was a fag?" Dad then knelt down beside me. "Were you hoping to be a ballerina?"

I shook my head. I sucked in my lower lip and began to hyperventilate.

Mom interrupted. "I bought these downtown at an outlet. Do you know how much those normally cost?" she asked, snatching my shame in the form of the pants from my father. "Do you know how cute they look on him?"

He paused for a moment, until the sign of eureka came across his face. "Well, he doesn't like them, so he'll wear some other fucking costume."

Dad used the word "costume" a lot. It made him sound like a hip Mafioso.

I said in between uncontrollable breaths, "But they're all like that."

Mom circled for a new angle. "He is the best-dressed boy in school, by far. All the other mothers think so." She seemed to swell with pride.

Without another word, Dad turned around and walked into my room. My room was where I could do whatever I wanted: food under the bed, games and puzzle pieces littered everywhere, and the last weeks' worth of clothes all over the floor. He flung open the closet door and pulled all my costumes out, emptied the contents of every drawer, and launched the entire mass onto my unmade bed. It was a sea of bright colors, ruffles, buckles, oversized buttons, all attached to a wardrobe of bygone days.

He took inventory of the clothes before him. He scoffed at the suspenders. "What is he, Fred Astair?" and then rolled his eyes at the street-scenes-of-Venice print shirts. His expression became more stunned with every passing moment and when he finally spoke, he sounded genuinely confused. "This is a complete joke, right?" Dad said, still looking into the morass of undersized clown uniforms.

My mother made a final attempt to put a positive spin on the whole episode. "These are really beautiful clothes," she said.

"This is complete bullshit! You know he is a kid, a boy. Right?" My hyperventilation slowed.

Dad handed me my pajama bottoms, which I pulled over my skinny legs. He then grabbed my arm hard and pulled me down the hall. As we left, my mother hummed an Eastern European dirge—usually only heard from her during times of stress—which followed us out the front door.

I sat in the front seat of Dad's red-and-white Volkswagen bus and stared out the window, my cheeks not yet dry from all my blubbering. I wondered where we were going.

"You must have taken a few beatings over some of them costumes," Dad said.

I did not answer right away. My mind drifted to all the evenings I sat in my room by myself with the door closed.

"It's not too bad," I said. A long silence followed, and I continued my gaze out the window. I imagined a whole host of future scenarios filled with ass-kicking from the playground and my mother, who was going to be pissed.

When we pulled into the parking lot, my dad's face changed again. His lips curled in, his eyes focused on something in the distance. I only saw this face when there was hell to pay. A face saved only for "special events," produced only after too many cans of Budweiser. Although I had seen this face many times, it never ceased to strike fear into me.

As much as I loved him, he scared me, and I began to cry again.

Dad said nothing, focusing instead upon the horizon as I sniffled away. He suddenly slammed the car into park, tearing the gearshift knob off and causing everything to lurch forward. My father then angrily spun around toward me. "I will ask you again… Are you taking a beating at school?"

I was too scared not to answer. "Yes, I get picked on all the time. I don't know what to do. I don't want to go to school anymore. I hate it. Don't make me go." Everything around me blurred from my tears, and it all came out, all the bullying, fear, and girly clothes that made me different from everyone else. As I talked, I felt relieved, but also like a coward for not knowing how to defend myself. Dad would never have been in this position, would never be picked on or be forced to dress like a loser.

Dad listened without blinking. The pause before he spoke prodded my return to hyperventilating. The springs in Dad's seat creak after he shifted.

"After we get you some new costumes, I will show you some stuff in the yard. Tomorrow, you're going to school and then you're getting in a fight." He looked out the windshield while tapping out a cigarette of a mostly crushed pack of Salem regulars and lit it. "If you don't do what I tell you to do, I am going to knock the shit out of you. Am I understood?" He turned back to me, pushed his lower lip out, and exhaled smoke to the van's ceiling.

I nodded yes.

Before the day was over, I had a new wardrobe. It was Dad's clothes, only smaller: boots, sweatshirts, Toughskin jeans, and white tube socks with two blue stripes at the top. All muted colors, so I blended. He said, "Wear gray and walk against the wall."

To this day, there is nothing like an oversized gray sweatshirt to make me feel comfortable.

After I changed, Dad demanded we meet in the backyard. I stood there in front of him posed like the boxers we saw on television. The next several hours were all about "old-school street fighting," as he put it. While he realized I didn't have the strength or coordination to do much of what he showed me, especially not while shaking in terror, he made a particular point to explain end-game strategy. "When you see the teachers coming to break up the fight, don't stop. When the teachers tell you to stop, don't. When they try to pull you off, hold on tighter. Scream to draw a crowd and don't let go no matter what.

Don't worry about how you look or what other people think. If you taste blood, you're doing it right. Don't worry that you're going to kill him. You won't." Dad smiled and continued. "You're just going to give him and everyone in earshot something to think about. No one wants to fuck with a crazy person." He put a comforting arm around me and then said, "Tomorrow, you fight. You have my word no one will ever bother you again. Or you will have to deal with me." Then he smiled. It was warm and gooey and felt safe. If I could have eaten anything I would have thrown it up.

The following day at lunch, per Dad's instructions, with tears rolling down my face, I ran up behind the biggest kid in the school, David Malmud, and tackled him from behind, small stones jabbing into my back as we rolled on the ground. I got behind him and grabbed his cheeks with both hands. The plan terrified me, but I was far more terrified of my father if I didn't do this right. I slid my first two fingers of each hand into the corners of David's mouth. It was easier than I thought, just like Dad had said. He called it "the fishhook."

Then I pulled up and back as hard as I could, trying to "pull the fucking kid's face off his head," just like Dad told me. David, and then I, both began to scream. I felt the tension in my arms, back, and stomach. I began to vibrate from my force. David swung his arms wildly in hopes that they would hit me, but I didn't let go. He grabbed at my hands. I felt my fingernails dig into the insides of David's cheeks. I heard him whimper and felt his saliva drip down my arm. I held my breath. When a teacher yelled at me to stop, I didn't let go.

I would mark this moment as the first time I ever felt in control. The first time I stood up for myself. I don't know how long it lasted, but when it was over, the whole school had encircled us, slack-jawed, and several teachers and Wally the janitor all held me down.

Tears and dirt and blood all mixed in my mouth.

It tasted like power.

That evening, Dad scolded me in front of Mom, using phrases like "what the fuck is wrong with you" and "you should fucking know better." Privately, when Mom was in the kitchen humming a Russian

song, Dad put his hand on my shoulder and said, "I'm proud of you."
Dad was right—rarely did I get picked on again.

But I remained scared of everything.

***

AFTER THE SCHOOLYARD FISHHOOK fight, Dad began to talk to
me differently. He swore more in front of me—which, at the time,
didn't seem possible. He treated me more like one of the guys. I liked
this. He wanted to toughen me up so I wouldn't look so much like
a chump. At least that's how I saw it. To his credit, he never verbally
confirmed my fears, but he started taking me out of our boring
Jewish neighborhood into downtown, where he worked with a red-
handled Milwaukee Sawzall and blue-handled channel locks. Tools
that looked like they were built for tough men. On Saturdays and in
the summers, he dragged me along for the ride.

The corner that sticks out in my mind is Alvarado and Eighth.
Noisy street vendors sold colorful shaved ice out of small freezers on
roller skates, a bell chiming on top. Round Latina ladies with small
broods in tow yelled as the traffic encroached into crosswalks. Cars
honked at each other, which sounded like an endless dialogue in a
foreign language. The corner held a morass of random guys, some
leaning on lampposts and wearing stained wifebeaters stretched over
their ballooning bellies. Shoeless crazies ran screaming, gurgling,
and barking through uncaring crowds, urgently heading to wherever
crazy people secretly went. Shop owners in smudged aprons watched
the whole uneasy parade from the relative quiet of their doorways.

Dad wanted to lift off the lid to life for me and show me its
flailing innards. Like I said, he cared about me, but wanted someone
more savvy and streetwise. As Dad and I walked, I wanted nothing
more than to strap myself to his leg for safety. Instead, he made sure
to point out every person of interest as if it were a game.

"See him?" Dad whispered in my ear. "Watch out for that fucking
guy." And he nodded in a general direction without pointing. "Watch
how he's looking around, like he's spying on something. He is either
surveying the landscape..." Dad took a meaningful drag on his cigarette.

"The landscape?" I asked.

"Yeah, he is looking for someone to rob. Someone who looks vulnerable or weak. Either that or he is trying to keep a low profile because he might have jacked the wrong guy." Dad's eyes darted back and forth, picking up tiny, scary details. He seemed to drool over dubious characters lurking in shadows.

He pointed at aged orange splatters on the cement and then up to the roof of the adjacent building. My eyes followed his finger all the way to the top edge of the building as he crouched and leaned in tight to me. "I saw this guy a couple of weeks ago do a swan dive, just like in the Olympics. I was standing just over there." He turned and pointed to the other side of the street. "He was walking across the roof like he was on a tight rope. People crowded around. And then—" Dad pointed back up to the roof "—the guy looks like he's bouncing on a springboard facing us. And then he just jumps."

Dad stood up and walked across the orange splatter as if it were not there.

Over time, I learned where all the orange splatters were, how to keep my chin up when I walked, how to walk with purpose so I never looked lost, and also how to pass Dad the tools with the colored handles when he needed them.

He was a plumber, and I found it magical. His hands were covered with knots and red places and torn skin. He told me that he would rip my arms out if I ever followed in his footsteps, which only made me like his tools more.

He said the same thing to me when military recruiters started calling the house when I turned eighteen. "Hey, loony tunes, do you like your fucking arms?" he called from his bedroom once when he heard me answer the phone and say, "Uh. Hello, Sergeant Smith..."

We left the chaos of the street and entered an empty apartment or basement. The outside world shut down until Dad broke out the wall to get at a pipe or switched on an electric drain snake for a clogged line. The grinding, banging, and brute force required to fix plumbing problems felt primal. My workday with Dad consisted of sitting cross-legged next to a pile of tools, handing him a wrench, blowtorch, or pipe cutter while he crammed himself in an awkward position on his back next to a rusty pipe. Most of the time, I watched quietly.

Dad said, "Work with wood, or some other fucking thing. Learn to build. Trust me, women love it." He put his filth-covered hand on my shoulder. "Learn to fix things, but plumbing? Leave that for the fucking idiots. The work is too hard."

It was not the act of sitting in a cramped space to see him fish out something disgusting from a drain that made it great for me. It was traveling to and from the job. He worked in a lot of neighborhoods that had character. I got a vicarious thrill of accomplishment walking through the fear of what I knew was a dodgy part of town. I still have an odd fondness for old blood stains on cement.

Downtown Los Angeles in the 1970s had an edge to it, and I was afraid of everything. Dad had an ability to walk through the crowded, clanging streets with a careless cool. He always had his wits about him, pointing out the marks, hustlers, junkies, and thieves without second-guessing himself. It all made sense. He was a street guy. He came from the south side of Chicago—from the baddest part of town, I assumed.

After jobs, Dad and I went into any store I wanted, both of us smelling of old metal tools. Dingy bookstores with peeling wood paneling selling mildewed comic books were my favorites, but I also loved auto part stores where everything smelled of rubber, or household junk stores, which resembled what normal stores would look like after an earthquake. Then we went to Orange Julius for a drink. We rarely spoke on the way home until after I had slurped down all the orange chemicals from the styrofoam cup and made the straw gurgle on the emptiness.

Dad then said something like, "How'd you like to live over there? If you want, I could turn around and dump you on one of the corners." And then he would make a fast turnaround one of the blocks.

He laughed all the way home.

I remember fighting one night with my mother when I was about fourteen. I said the word "fuck" in a sentence directed toward her. Dad walked into the room and grabbed me by the arm, walked me out the front door, and threw me into the car. He drove down

Sixth Street while I pressed my cheek against the cold passenger's side window and ignored anything he said. We eventually drove in silence except for K-Earth, the station for keeping fifties and early sixties music alive, until we pulled over to a corner around Alameda and stopped. The night's cold chilled me when Dad got out of the car. He stomped around the front of the car and unlocked my side and opened the door. He pulled me out and then shut the door as I shrugged him off of me. Around us there was nothing but a few streetlamps, boarded-up shops, fencing topped with razor wire. About a block away, I could see a small orange fire with a couple of figures warming themselves in front of it.

Dad walked back around the front of the car and hopped into the driver's seat. I was confused, looked at him quizzically through the glass. He said, "If you don't like it where you're at, stay the fuck here!" He turned on the ignition, turned on the headlights, and drove away. For the first minute, I looked around as if it were a joke. I mean surely a skinny, drippy crybaby like myself should not be stranded on a deserted street, right?

My heart pounded so hard I thought it would explode as I watched the red taillights of Dad's van turn the corner and disappear. I had no money and no jacket. The cold nibbled at the tops of my bare arms, reminding me how pencil thin they were as they poked out of my cheap white T-shirt. I had a habit of chewing on the neck of my T-shirt, and this one hung lifeless, all the elasticity sucked out of it.

A guy leaning against a graffiti-covered building across the street watched the whole scene but stood there unimpressed. I tried to breathe slowly, to calm myself. When I felt the guy across the street staring at me, I started to walk.

I stayed in the middle of the empty street, under the safety of the streetlamps, frequently but nonchalantly looking behind me. I walked close to the fire. Not near enough to feel its warmth, but near enough to see the two men. They were both black, wore ragged clothes, and did not acknowledge my existence, which was fine by me.

I knew I was being punished, but it was thrilling. Whatever sense of danger I think Dad expected me to feel, I felt—only more so. I stood there for a moment and drank it in.

Moreover, nothing horrible was happening. Nobody came with a net or a knife gleaming in the moonlight. Nobody dragged me into a windowless van or tried to rob me. I stood in the glorious, terrifying void until I saw two flashes of lights behind me.

It was Dad's van.

Dad smoked a cigarette and looked straight ahead. Through the glass, he said, "Get in before I change my mind." The stereo played "Runaround Sue" as we drove home wordlessly, Dad staring ahead and me staring at his hands.

***

AFTER A COUPLE WEEKS of silence, Cathy called to tell me she needed to meet me and had enough gas money to make the trip from St. George to Los Angeles. We met at the Farmer's Daughter Hotel on Fairfax Avenue and across the street of the farmers market. It was Dad's motel and his motel of choice when his family came to town. The place was a dump historically, but the new owners had painted it dark blue and made its restaurant hip after the megamall across the street was built.

I was always surprised at my willingness to get behind the wheel and drive to a place I did not want to be out of a sense of obligation. I arrived numb, more confused than sad over Dad's death and not at all interested in making new friends. We met in the parking lot. Cathy wore a pink jumpsuit, which matched her phony, bright pink nails exactly. She was plump and blonde with her hair pulled back into a ponytail. She smiled at me, and I tried to smile back. I wore blue shorts and flip-flops and a baggy T-shirt. Everything on me was loose. I had stopped eating.

My jaw clicked from the tension in my face when I said hello, and she gave me an awkward hug, or I awkwardly received it. I then stood there with my hands in my pockets wondering whether we were to sort our issues with Dad, or what? Little did I know Cathy would stay a week.

I said to Cathy, "It is really a pleasure," which was not remotely true, but it was all I had. My stomach gurgled and churned. My throat got tight. I wanted to barf, but I held a residual sense of duty toward

Dad and felt compassion for Cathy. I knew that Cathy wanted
something from me. I just did not know what.

Our meetings blurred together from lunch and dinner and chats
and my sluggishness. I shared the details of my life and my heavily
edited memories of my father, because there had to be a positive
spin, but mostly I listened.

"I really miss him," she said over and over, with a smile that
came from love. Each time she looked almost surprised by her
acknowledgement. As if his death had not sunk in. She told me about
their long talks and how he made her laugh. Her eyes misted many
times during her visit. She shared he was still floating around their
trailer they shared in St. George. She'd told him, "Okay, honey, you
can stay for a little bit, but you have to get ready to go home to Cádiz."

Then she looked skyward.

Cádiz? I thought.

"Cádiz is a city along the Mediterranean Sea in Spain," she
explained. "All I know is he wanted to go home to Cádiz."

The statement was curious. *What home?* I thought. He never
lived in Spain, at least not that I knew of. He didn't fly. He wasn't a
boat guy. I scratched my head. "When was he in Spain?" I asked.

"Well, you must have known," she said with her ponytail pulled
askew. "He talked about it all the time. He lived up a hill by a crooked
tree," she said.

It all smelled of bullshit, but I kept my thoughts to myself.

"Maybe he wanted me to take him there. Maybe he just wanted
me to see Spain with him. He was a good man." Cathy looked to
the side and let out a soft sigh and cradled her head on her hand.
I squirmed in my seat.

Good man? Cádiz? I should have asked more questions.

She handed me a Polaroid photo of him looking aged and
disheveled, wearing a hospital gown and a chrome halo glued to his
head, sort of like a lampshade without the shade. He looked lonely
and weary. "One day we were driving and he just started shaking and
flipping out. That's how we learned about the brain tumors." She told
me about his hospital stays. "We all thought that the brain would get
him. No one saw the heart attack coming," she said.

I handed the photograph back to her as quickly as I could.

The day before Cathy left, we sat quietly in my car next to a park, underneath a big shade tree, all talked out. We were listening to the birds and kids playing in the distance when Cathy said, "You know, he told me about the storage unit."

She said it like it were code. I looked at her, expecting more to the story. She stared at me, waiting for *me* to elaborate.

I said, "What storage unit?"

She crossed her arms and looked out the passenger window and let out a heavy sigh. "You know the one. The one where the statue of Brigham Young is pointing. That big Mormon Church and the statue is pointing at the storage unit. You know the storage unit," she said, and she turned toward me and tilted her head in an attempt to will me to understand, or more likely to come clean.

I said nothing.

"Okay," she said, "your dad said that you knew all about it. There was the storage unit and that you knew the combination to the lock. He said you had lots of storage units, but this one was important. Remember. In the back. Behind the tarp?" She waved her arms as if to pull aside an invisible tarp to help guide me along. She continued, "Not the crate to the left, but underneath the empty crate on the right. Do you remember now?"

It was like Dad to offer specific directions to the treasure but vagueness about his prizes. Cathy said nothing about what was supposed to be in the crates—gold bars, masterpiece paintings, stacks of cash. Dad left that to the imagination.

All I could do was shake my head, while Cathy waited, looking at me like I was playing dumb. I knew she suspected that there must be a treasure in the crate and that it was rightfully hers but I had beaten her to it, that I must have swindled her out of her fair share of the fortune.

Dad was an expert of the short con, but his long play was much more powerful. I assumed he developed a story that, even in death, would make it look like he would always take care of her. He never wanted to be the goat for breaking her heart, and leaving her without a future, so Dad sold stories. How she must have felt giving him her youth and left, in the end, with memories of an adventure, which is maybe the best we can ever get. And through it all, I was jealous. She had him all that time.

"I did not know of any storage unit, or crates, or anything of value hidden by the statue of Brigham Young, or any place else." I tried to explain more about the dad I knew. I said, "I think he wanted you to know that you had a future that he just could not provide. He must have loved you a lot, but he pissed through a small fortune in Vegas."

I don't think she believed me.

I later drove down Santa Monica Boulevard and around the Mormon Church looking for a storage unit place or a garage where Dad might have left crates of money for me and Cathy.

There was none.

In the years that followed, Cathy crept into my mind often. I assumed her final years with Dad must have been total crap, but she stayed with him. She stayed with him while she pushed carts together in the local town market parking lot.

He was old. His looks had faded. He was bloated and chain-smoking with brain tumors and seizures and absolutely zero dollars, all the while lying to her about a secret stash of money that would surely belong to her one day. I saw him as a million empty packs of cigarettes crushed into alleyway litter and scattered aimlessly across the asphalt. There must have been years when Dad's charming shtick finally stopped working altogether—not because he was no longer smart, but because he had given up. I saw it in his face that last time in the 7-Eleven parking lot. I felt it as he dropped the brass elephant in my lap and it crushed my nuts. It was impossible not to see what that life must have looked like to Dad from the rusted, cramped trailer in St. George, his world held together with bungee cords, electrical tape, and stories. The idea made me sick, but Cathy stuck by him.

Dad was lucky to have her, and briefly, I felt compassion.

I was around two years sober and spent a fair amount of time looking to make conscious acts of honesty, but in my heart, I know that if there had been a treasure, I would have never shared it. A day later, Cathy drove back to St. George, Utah, with less than she'd left with—namely his medical records and a huge, bright yellow envelope filled with X-rays of Dad's brain tumors, just in case there was something wrong inside my head too.

***

MONTHS AFTER HIS DEATH, Dad still lived in some abyss in my head, showing up in my dreams or participating in fairly realistic, two-sided conversations while I did the dishes. I had been working an extended gig in Las Vegas, one of Dad's favorite haunts, at the time. Vegas was a miserable place to live in the summer. I remembered walking through the automatic double doors, which led from frosty air-conditioned casinos into invisible packets of flaming photons that seared my face like brimstone. Everything looked as though washed in red and my eyes burned all the time, but the money was good.

The job was as a location scout on a big-budget commercial, and I had settled into three months of Vegas culture, paperwork, and meetings with city and county officials. My days of drinking and gambling were long over. I was single for the first time in years and stayed off the strip in one of the few hotels in Vegas without gaming, my temporary home away from home.

During my stay, the hotel hosted a parade of organizations and events: the world championships of yo-yo followed by an odd fourteen-year-olds' cheerleading event. Then came the computer hackers' convention, also known as Def-Con, Lustfest, and so on. No matter who came to town, I never fit in with the spirit of the hotel, or of Vegas.

Unfortunately, I was transitioning in my life and working for a real blowhard, who did very much embody the spirit.

"Yo, D, come here a minute." It was my boss, Jerry.

Jerry wore brown loafers without socks and Oxford shirts that were bursting at the buttons from his distended stomach. He had dark wavy hair, a stubbled chin, a small purple potato for a nose, and wore sunglasses at dusk. When we worked in his office, which was his hotel room on that job, he usually wore only a loose-fitting towel around his waist, his ass crack somehow visible from every direction—even facing forward. His voice boomed in a way that suggested professionalism was his top priority. I disliked him from day one but resolved to make the most of things.

And so I hung with him, standing by a table of drunken honeymooners playing fifteen-dollar blackjack at the Venetian Hotel with my hands in my pockets, trying not to count the cards but doing it anyway. A previous incarnation of myself would have been escorted out by the pit bosses by now, but times had changed.

I was comfortable with my life now, even if I was not always comfortable with me.

My boss wanted a drink, and he wanted me to accompany him so he didn't have to drink alone. I was a terrible wingman. Vegas depressed me. The casino world, I had decided, had changed. The accountants took over for the mobsters and made gaming, eating, shopping, or having fun in Vegas cost-prohibitive—or maybe it was just me.

"Yo, D," Jerry called again. I walked over to the Venetian's octagonal bar. It was a slow weeknight in the casino. Slack-jawed zombie people milled about, but without the roar of craps-table excitement or incessant ponging of the slots, the place felt deflated. My boss leaned on the railing with a beer and an Asian woman, who was obviously a prostitute. She was tall and thin—early thirties, I guessed. She was the kind of skinny that grinds its teeth even in the afternoon. As I walked up, Jerry said, "This lovely has a question for you."

She said something I couldn't make out through her thick Chinese accent. I turned to Jerry, who clarified, "This lovely one is Audrey," and he put his arm around her teeny waist. Audrey had frosted hair and caked-on aqua-marine eye shadow. She wore tight jeans and a fake alligator belt with pink suede boots. Her bowling-ball implants heaved against her button-down shirt as she coyly batted long, phony lashes at me and said something that sounded like, "Hello, how would you like to roll on the bed with my friend?" and I waited for Jerry to translate.

I faced her with my hands on my hips like I was ready to start a steeple-chase and bolt at the first chance. I had a lot on my mind. Cathy had called a couple of days earlier, her voice small and defeated:

"I think your dad wanted me to go to Spain for him," she said. "With him," she corrected herself. "But I don't think it is going to happen. Money's tight, you know."

She was broke, more broke than I was. The likelihood of her winning the lottery or saving enough cash for the trip to Spain was slim. At the same time, once I knew Dad's final wish was to be scattered off the coast of Spain, I felt I was the only person who could stake claim to that job. Cathy had moved in with another guy already. A biker guy or a truck driver, I thought. She was still in St. George. Still working at the market, too, and I did not want to have any more information than that. Perhaps I thought she moved on too quickly, and perhaps it had taken me far too long.

Either way, I'd earned the right to scatter that jackass.

So I stood in front of an overly painted prostitute and thought about my dead father and his ashes. His final wish would now be officially my problem.

Cathy had said, "I really want to take him, but I know I might never be able to. You know. And I think you probably might make it one day. Your dad said you're really resourceful. Maybe you can come get him, and make sure you take an awful lot of pictures of Cádiz for me." As I was feeling progressively more awful for Cathy, a young blonde hooker appeared at the other prostitute's side.

The blonde posed with her hand on her hip, open-mouthed, with small blue eyes, and she wore a red formfitting tube dress without a hint of underpants. She was no more than twenty-two. "Really a pleasure. I'm Charlotte," she said, extending her hand like royalty and throwing in a half curtsy for good measure. I took her hand, and she turned a full circle and squealed with glee as she wrapped my arm around her. She took a moment to gyrate into my pelvis before spinning back out and finished with another curtsy. It was a dance move that she had practiced well. Then she pulled me to her and whispered into my ear, "I want you." She stroked my hand, licking her lips, and staring alternately into my eyes and crotch, and Jerry said to the ladies, "Do you mind if I chat with my partner?"

He looked back and forth to both women.

I looked behind me to see where his partner was.

He took me by the arm and pulled me out of Charlotte's grip and walked me over to that dead casino game with the giant spinning wheel.

Once we were out of earshot, Jerry said, "So, what do you think?" then he looked back at Audrey and Charlotte, who sent come-hither winks and blew kisses at us.

I said, "I think they're both retarded, but I think yours is the worse of the two."

"No, what do you really think?" he said. He then smiled toward them, nodding his head.

"Really," I said, "I think they are both retarded."

Off to the side, bells chimed to announce a jackpot.

"Well," Jerry said, "I think Audrey and Charlotte are a pair and they come as a package deal. They want eight hundred bucks for the two of them. What do you think?"

I thought about dumping Charlotte at a shelter for runaways. I thought about getting Audrey in a headlock and scrubbing her face clean with lava soap and a steel wool pad. Mostly, I thought about getting out of Vegas.

"No, dude, I am not in," I said.

I was—am—no saint, but a wave of judgment filled me. I am also really cheap. Besides, this was Vegas. There were about a million drunken women running around waiting to have a story to tell, but Jerry did not want to work that hard. I moralized myself above the trappings of Vegas. I had moved beyond the gambling and drinking but not beyond obnoxious self-righteousness.

Jerry put his hands to his head in exasperation. "How much petty cash do you have in your room?" he asked, and before I could answer, he continued, "Okay, so I am going to take them both. So we'll go back to the room. You'll go to your room and get the eight hundred. No, make that nine—I think the Chink will take it in the ass. Then you come back to my room with us and hang for a little while."

I threw my hands out while I flung my head and shouted at the ceiling. "What for?" I said. "I am ready to take a nap. How about I drop off the money and split immediately, good? I don't need to be there." I was okay with him using the money that we needed to administer a huge commercial, but hanging around with Jerry and the hookers for another fifteen minutes seemed unreasonable.

Jerry looked down and shook his head. "Naw, man, I have to take a huge shit. I can't have them sitting around in my room by themselves." I grumbled to myself and paced in a small circle. I felt like a weasel for not quitting on the spot. He was distracted and said, "It's settled then." He and I walked back to the prostitutes and he said, "So, babies, how about we party?"

I sat quietly as fluorescent lights bounced off the windshield on the cab ride back to the hotel. Jerry and the hookers laughed up a storm.

At the hotel, I made small talk with the girls while Jerry took a crap that shook the walls and created a palpable stink, easily outmatching the ceiling fan above our heads. Charlotte pulled out one impressive breast, double-checking my commitment to not fucking her.

"It's quite lovely," I said. And it was.

I guessed she wanted no part of Jerry.

Charlotte tucked away her boob and sat on the couch next to Audrey. Both seemed oblivious to the stench that seeped through the walls. Jerry emerged like a breaching whale wearing aftershave that smelled like Pine Sol and said, "Ladies! Heh, heh, heh."

I gave Jerry $1,000 in petty cash and leaned in to remind him that I was not responsible if there was a problem repaying the till. Before I went to sleep, I jerked off thinking about Charlotte's one impressive breast. Then I dreamt about the awful trailer park my dad died in. In the morning, I would drive to St. George and see Cathy one last time.

Chapter 2

CATHY GREETED ME LIKE an old friend in the trailer park where she and Dad lived. I felt nothing. The ride up from Vegas had me thinking about why. Why Dad disappeared. I wish I could say that we had some major falling out, but I can't. He and Mom divorced when I was twenty, and he left for good. It was not entirely surprising. I always remember him as a drifter at heart, a Boxcar Willie–type always looking for a joyride to parts unknown, but I never expected a mobile home in the desert with cinder block steps and shag carpet that reeked of cigarettes.

And then eighteen years after that, here were Cathy and I lunching and chatting about her family, me struggling to pay attention and mostly wanting to leave from the moment I had arrived. After Cathy gave me Dad's ashes, I placed them in the front seat of my car. He was in a small, brown vinyl satchel with drawstrings on it. I stared out at the Red Rock Mountains and considered the journey back to Los Angeles, the miles that lay ahead.

The plan was to have one final talk, to catch up, no matter how one-sided it might be. The man-to-man talk that was so long overdue. I would talk about the parts of my life he missed, as there were many. I would tell him all about what became of his family. Maybe throw in a few anecdotes about old friends. I turned the ignition, revved the engine, looked down at the leather bag that contained my father, and realized there would be no talk. Regardless of my personal belief in a thriving spirit world, he was no longer here. And more importantly, I had nothing to say.

After I returned home from St. George and Vegas, things were supposed to go back to normal. Instead, I checked the refrigerator every fifteen minutes, paced the living room, missed sleep, checked my email compulsively—anything to avoid Dad and the strange pang of honoring him biting at my heels. He was a jerk, after all.

Guilt finally won out several weeks later, and I decided that Dad needed a funeral. Well, that I needed to have a funeral for him. A funeral is one of those customs both appropriate and barbaric to me. There is something to be said for celebrating those we love by feeling sad in a group and taking a moment to say flowery things about life and death. However, it is also a fuss and an expense, and perhaps I understood why Dad wanted nothing to do with the ritual.

At the same time, I have often wondered if Dad's decision to go without a funeral had more to do with being alienated by and owing money to most of his family. I wondered if he thought no one would show up or say something nice about him. Still I wanted something for me, a chance to say goodbye. I imagined it as celebration of the contributions he had made on this planet—at least the positive ways he had influenced me.

I might have made the drive to St. George, Utah, to pay my respects under the willow tree and wear black. I imagined myself sitting cross-legged by his gravesite attempting to ask questions. Even in my imagination, though, there was nothing more than the breeze or far-off birds chirping. None of my questions would be answered, but the ritual has a way of washing a situation clean, even if a funeral in St. George would have been foreign and unfamiliar to me.

I wanted to have the funeral my way, in familiar surroundings, as a way to have some control over him beyond simply saying goodbye. I wanted something to acknowledge that I was upset by Dad's death, and I wanted to be purified. However, in hindsight, I also wanted to get sympathy for the way Dad disassociated himself from me and died in a rusted-out trailer, cigarette still burning in his hand, in a section of town that I can only charitably describe as "lowend." A place the dad I knew would have described as a "fucking shithole filled with idiots." I wanted a cosmic apology from him living his life differently than what I wanted. Or I wanted tears from my friends for my grief.

There had to be a funeral.

***

THE LIGHTS HAD BEEN dimmed and several candles lit. It was dusk, and the golden light cast warm shadows through the cracks between the drapes. A single white rose sat on the altar I had made out of low-grade plywood and painted black.

My fellow initiates sat in a half moon on a variety of mismatched chairs. We wore white ceremonial robes and sat in silence until I stood up and placed the brown sack with Dad's ashes in it next to the white rose. I can only imagine what my father would have said.

I assumed Dad had received an ethereal invitation to the event and was floating at the top of the room as a puff of smoke, looking down with his arms folded across his chest, trying to make sense of the scene. Dad, while not a caveman philosophically, would not have seen much value in my occult sensibilities. I stood and walked to the west side of the altar, lighting a big pinch of pungent incense. The sharp odor filled the room.

My friends and I were all bent on celebrating the life of my father (who would have thought them all idiots) and helping me mourn the loss of Dad (who would have also thought me an idiot). This memory is firm. I had moved far, far away from Dad's Catholic roots. He grew up surrounded by robed nuns who demanded unquestioning obedience while he wore schoolboy short pants and embraced the Virgin Mary.

Once, growing up, I asked, "Dad, what is God?"

He'd been on his way out of the living room, shaking a brown bottle of Maalox. He turned back with bloodshot eyes. "You want to know about God? You want to know about religion?" he said, standing there in striped boxers and looking as if I'd threatened him. "Expect beatings and poverty. It is all the same fucking deal." Then he stopped in the doorway. "Do you want a beating? I could give you one."

He unscrewed the white metal cap and took a long sip of Maalox that left a chalky white film on the top of his mouth.

I shook my head.

Even with Dad's disdain, I went off seeking God in my late twenties. Over the years, I had sat in churches, mosques, and synagogues. I pranced in a weed-cluttered backyard with a chubby pagan in stretch pants named Raven. I donated my time, attempted confession, wore crystals, chanted, prayed, and chakrah-ed my way through most every spiritual and religious dogma possible, finally ending up with a small group that was one part secret society, one part archaic mysticism, and one part high-school-popularity-contest losers. I liked its socially progressive leanings and one-hundred-year-old esoteric writings by Victorian snobs that tried to explain the universe in a cohesive formula that could be used by all. I gave them a B minus in content but an A plus in intellectual superiority. I decided that understanding God was a pursuit for those who had too much time on their hands, but not that day. I wanted a sign. I wanted the burning bush that made me tremble in my boots, if only for a little proof that there was some great beyond with Dad holding court in it.

Now, the eldest woman stood in front of the altar with her short gray hair and glasses, raising her arms to the sky. She led a creative visualization about my father being in a happy place and some mentions of me seeing him finally crossing over the veil to walk amongst the light. "Go into the light," we cajoled the sack with Dad in it. "Go into the light."

Surely the chanting would piss him off enough to comment.

I closed my eyes and waited for an image of Dad flying Superman-style into a vortex of halogen light bulbs. I got nothing, and I started to cry anyway. It was a good one. I opened my mouth and started to ramble on about Dad and my extra special relationship with him. It was sincere, but not accurate. True or not, they all sat there and witnessed. The men watched and focused meditatively. The women put their arms around me and gave me what I needed: the validation for a boy who lost his father. It was all so sentimental. I was conscious enough to be grateful.

Sure, it was silly, but no sillier than any other ritual that required an unseen world and old white men as prophets. It was here that I first truly examined the afterlife with clear goggles. It was a moment that offered me comfort and trauma. There I was, crying about my father and the light of heaven.

Then I heard my father's voice.

Not the kind of fantastical voice that foretells fear or a diagnosis of a psychotic break, but the kind of familiar parental voice that weaves its way into a child's thoughts and never quite fades away. The voice clanged, both scolding and comforting, with a practical sensibility and a way of cutting through the nonsense.

Dad said, "What kind of bullshit is this? You're sitting in a dress. Do you really get laid in a costume like this? Would you put on some pants?"

"It's a ceremonial garment," I argued. "It's sacred."

"Why don't you just put out a few pictures of your father up around the house and move on with your life, you fucking idiot."

I was torn. I wanted to embrace the hopeful fable that Dad and I would one day meet again, perhaps as blooming flowers planted in the same soil, or two tree frogs on a really low branch; however, I began to have my doubts about all of it. I wanted all that stuff about religious immortality and a watchful God to be true, because having to think about the end being just an end and nothing else was a total drag. There would be no white light during the rite. I sniffled and pondered what it would be like when everything just stopped. No reincarnation, no dispersing, no knowing bullfrogs on low-hanging limbs, just unconscious nothingness.

A few hours later, my pagan friends and I went to Koo Koo Roo's, a quick-serve, faux-health joint, to discuss the Tree of Life and other esoteric things and eat roasted chicken slathered in an addicting house sauce. Between the genuine tears of sadness and the nagging headache that comes from fighting such tears, I thought about whether it was possible to remember only the good and simply let go of the bad. Later that night, a future ex blew me in the living room while I thought about whether the funeral accomplished anything at all.

***

THE NEXT DAY I threw Dad on the dresser in my bedroom and left him there for several years. There was no "Ave Maria," no Cádiz, no gaggles of mourning, black-laced señoritas. Occasionally I'd look up at him thinking, "One of these days I ought to..." but I had not lifted a finger to make his bullshit last request of returning him "home" to Spain come true.

The top of the dresser accidentally became a shelf for incomplete projects: the impulse-purchase mandolin that I never learned how to play, the family photo with the broken glass that needed reframing, the rainbow-colored set of paints—I don't even remember what I wanted to do with those—the incense burner that reminded me to meditate, two unfinished paperbacks, and a small box of unorganized receipts. It looked like a tiny garage sale from my unproductive life. Fortunately, the dresser was tall and kept failure out of view.

I am not sure what prompted the words one random afternoon, but I remember looking up at the brown vinyl bag and finally saying, "Okay, it's time for you to go."

I said it out loud. My voice sounded certain, which surprised me—and also convinced me. I was again penniless, and in-between jobs, but Dad was going home.

I dragged a green bentwood chair next to the dresser and pulled Dad down. He left a ring of bare wood where the dust could not reach. I plopped him on my bed and loosened the vinyl straps to help him breathe. Inside was a hermetically sealed, black plastic drum about a foot high, rectangular, with rounded corners and tapered at its base. It was small and sturdy. On the lid was Dad's full name: David Henry Galaudet. With the drum came official-looking transportation documents, which I had stuffed inside for safekeeping. Below these sat a Polaroid picture of his last family. I was surprised that I missed it when I added Dad's travel documents before I left Utah, and that Dad was not a pile of carbon and bits of bone in a sack.

Cathy was missing a couple of teeth. Sandy, who had graduated school, stood next to her new husband, Pete, who had just joined the army. His arm was around Sandy's younger sister, Kelly, a pending baby begin to show while she held the latest one in her arms. Kelly's guy friend, who wasn't the father to either baby, stood with his hands in his pockets. I had taken the Polaroid picture of them in front of Kentucky Fried Chicken, which was prominent in the photo's background. They had been nothing but nice to me, and I was still angry.

There had been a time when I would have stood atop Dad's pyramid. They had replaced me. I also knew calling them to sponsor a trip to scatter Dad was out of the question. I'd traded my film industry job for a hammer and a screw gun, but over the last few years I'd also written some travel articles for a trade publication read by travel agents. Up to that point, I had received a few free trips to write travel articles in-between construction jobs.

I loved writing but felt like a fraud. I lacked technical skills and much of a vocabulary; the use of the dreaded comma baffled me. Secretly, I imagined "real" writers would find out where I lived and stab me with pointy quills while I slept until poison ink flowed through my veins. However, until that happened, I tried hard to write well and planned to lobby for a trip to Spain.

I hoped to approach Spain's national tourism organization and plead for free airline tickets, room and board, and whatever else I needed in order to write a fifteen-hundred-word story about Flamenco dancing, small plates of food, or Picasso. It seemed like a long shot, but nothing better came to mind.

I also needed to justify the trip by getting the approval from the editor I was writing for. I made up an elaborate story about the importance of Spain to his readership and its importance to European history, but when he answered the phone, I told him the truth. "Hey there," I said, "my father has been dead, sitting on my dresser in a sack, for several years. I also discovered that I own a mandolin. He is supposed to be scattered in Spain somewhere off the coast of Cádiz. It all sounds like bullshit to me, but I promised I would do it. Can I write you a story or two about Spain if I can get them to pay for the whole thing?"

I tilted the phone's microphone away to hide my panicked breathing. I resisted the urge to say anything during the fifteen-second pause while the editor considered it. He said, "Here is the contact number for the Tourism Board of Spain. So sorry for your loss."

I called the number I'd been given moments after I hung up with my editor and scheduled a face-to-face with a woman who handled media relations for the Tourism Board of Spain in Los Angeles. Little did I know, this woman—Luciana—would change everything for me. I wore the one tattered suit I owned and stammered and perspired through a calm exterior while feeling like a thief, but good timing prevailed. Luck was on my side that day, and the Tourism Board of Spain needed a writer to report on a new series of operas that was to be held annually in Sevilla (since cancelled)—oddly enough the next major city closest to Cádiz—and I could get a story in a magazine they wanted to be featured in. We discussed my visiting Cádiz, and Luciana was happy to set up an additional week's worth of story scouting in Andalucia with a stop at Cádiz Tourism for my regional itinerary. Within moments, Dad went from covered with dust to something tangible and alive, something to smuggle.

With tickets in hand, I removed my shoes, belt, jacket, sunglasses, and cap and gathered my passport, traveler's checks, and a cell phone. I threw everything into several gray plastic tubs for security checkpoint examination. I waited in line and felt like a criminal. It is an odd circumstance that an organization like the Transportation Security Administration uses tactics that would be criminal in any other situation but have become routine in the name of freedom: limiting freedom during its clearance process. I took tiny steps in my stockinged feet along with everyone else. I placed my suitcase with Dad onto the conveyer belt with the rest of my belongings. I kept the official-looking "my father is dead" documents in my hand with my passport and boarding pass. Everything slid through the cruel beige X-ray machine.

Dad was never fond of the medical community, and X-rays were probably the last things that he ever wanted to have in his life. As the conveyor belt rolled, security folks began to mumble and point, and I knew my suitcase had come into view.

When my suitcase came out the other side, a mustachioed man wearing a light blue button-down shirt and a humorless expression grabbed my suitcase and marched it over to a shiny steel table. He grabbed the zippers and began to open the case. He tossed my loose pairs of underpants and socks aside to get at the plastic drum. I approached him and squealed in a high-pitched lady voice, "Hey, be careful!"

He took two steps back and pointed at me and said, "Sir, back away from the case!"

I raised both my hands, OK Corral–style, took two steps backward, and dropped the level of my voice ten decibels and an octave lower.

"Sir," I said, "that's my father in that plastic case. I'm taking his ashes to be scattered out of the country, I have some paperwork if you want to take a look at it." With my hands still raised, I waved the one that held my documents. I then slowly started to hand him my paperwork, which he did not look at, but lowered his head and said, "I'm really sorry to hear about your father, but I have to swab him. He might be a bomb."

The mustachioed security guy never did look at any of my paperwork. Neither did anybody else.

I sat down in my narrow coach seat, with Dad carefully smushed into the plane's overhead baggage, and wanted nothing more than to fall asleep. The airplane's pressurized cabin whirled and breezed, rolling metal carts carrying snacks and water clanged into my seat, the passenger next to me read with one of those airplane Alcatraz spotlights, and I restlessly reclined, sat up, readjusted the seat's pleather headrest, reclined, turned on my side, pulled my knees to my chest, and tried to rest my head on the tray table in front of me with the world's teensiest pillow. When nothing worked, I paced around the plane's aisles trying not to think about Dad.

***

"Don't worry, I'll still be kicking your ass when you're a hundred!" he said while he jabbed his nicotine-calloused finger against my bony chest. At seven years old, I found his threat comforting, and more importantly, I believed him. Dad stood in the glow of the refrigerator light in only striped boxers, which were all he ever wore when indoors. He had big arms and legs, a barrel chest, and thick, jabbing fingers. I could smell the cigarettes and Maalox on his breath, which was all he ever smelled like unless he had been drinking. Then he smelled like vegetables rotting in a garbage disposal, and this smell both frightened and thrilled me.

I wore the same powder-blue pajamas I had had since I was four. I was just as skinny as when they were first given to me. The bottoms came up to my shins and the top to my forearms. I never planned for more pajamas.

I had just cornered Dad in the service porch. Tears slathered down my face while I tried to explain what I was afraid of. Earlier that day in school, I had learned that smoking kills. My father smoked three packs of Salem menthols a day and, after the first, lit each one from the cherry end of the one he was still smoking. He was not in the mood for my blubbering.

I tried to tell him how glad I was that he would still be around for a long time. "Dad," I said, and then I started hyperventilating. It was times like these that I was certain that Dad wanted a son with a thicker skin. This thought only brought more tears.

Without another word, and with a look of exhaustion, he lumbered away. He took with him a huge tumbler of milk, half a loaf of white bread, and a cube of butter on his silver bedtime tray. I remember thinking he could unnerve the most steadfast of "belly-bucking champions," a term I learned from a show I had seen that pitted two shirtless fat guys against each other. They slammed stomachs for points, the same way bighorn rams proved alpha-male dominance in the wild but without the bellies or the points. Dad was my hero.

It was a relief to know that he was going to live to be at least a hundred and thirty, and his longevity made me feel better as I listened to him pound down the hallway. I had spent the early part of my life waiting for his departure, which happened often. My parents' volatile personalities resulted in slammed doors and Dad needing to "get out of Dodge." I had this image of him in my mind closing the front door behind him wearing a brown baker boy cap and his jacket collar turned up, holding a paper bag filled with jumbled clothes, and me in my same blue pajamas chasing after him toward the door—although I do not remember him ever owning a hat at any other time, ever. Sometimes he left without my mother's encouragement when "a couple of drinks" turned into days or a trip to Vegas without a trace. While he was gone, my mother and I would go on bottle hunts around the house for his alcohol, or go on welfare. Or she would hole herself up behind her bedroom door, leaving me on the other side.

I thought if I were a better son, Dad would come home and stay.

When Dad returned, he would simply materialize. No fanfare or explanation, just him there in the living room, smoking a cigarette, shirtless, in his tattered boxers, having a coffee. I would be overjoyed. Sometimes he pulled me off to the side in our small apartment and crouched down to my eye level. His aftershave burned my eyes and made them water. He told me complicated stories of being lost or locked up but always planning on coming back home. He'd say, "How could I not come for you." He hugged and kissed me. He apologized and promised no more yelling, or no more drinking, or no more leaving.

I would say, "Okay, no more Dr. Jekyll and Mr. Hyde?" He always agreed, and I wanted to believe that *this* time would be different, that he would stay for good. When I lay in bed and listened to my parents fight, though, I knew differently. There would be another day, another argument.

I stared at the ceiling under a dark blue haze and I knew there would be a day when Dad would be gone for good, but that seemed nebulous and far away, or not real—even if the knot in my stomach suggested otherwise.

✳✳✳

DAD WAS BORN TO a fertile mother who had thirteen children—including three sets of twins in a five-year span—and a nondescript, distant father who left the family after eleven of those children were born. When Dad, one half of the first set of twins, spoke about his childhood, the subjects ranged from poverty to religious disdain, petty crimes to grand larceny. He told stories that smacked of surviving by use of guile and cunning, and words like "success," "stability," and "future" never showed up. He said it all with a smile. He had a romantic relationship with his own history, which painted 1930s and '40s Chicago as a small town with rules that ran the street, rules he followed well or invented.

Coming from a poor family, Dad was never given the opportunities that came from social standing or money, but he knew how to hustle and was good with the tools he was given. He could fix a car with the metallic foil of a gum wrapper or hold court in a social gathering. He was smart and strong, with wide shoulders and hands, thick wrists, and bright blue eyes. My uncle Rick once said of Dad's physical gifts, "He should have been a prize fighter." Dad understood how to project confidence, and he lied with slyness. I, on the other hand, saw myself as too thin, like the shivering dog in the Haunted Mansion ride at Disneyland, all ribs and cowering.

As a kid, I was in awe. As an adult, envious.

***

OUR WHOLE APARTMENT SHOOK as Dad bounded down the hall to answer the phone. It was dark outside but still early in the evening due to Daylight Savings Time. Dad often mistook a dark outside as the middle of the night if he had a few drinks during the day and came home to sleep it off.

"Do you have a fucking clue what time it is?" he said to the caller. I heard a brief pause before, "Listen, motherfucker, I don't give a shit what you think you deserve."

It turned out Dad was speaking to Chiam, a portly man, who wore a yarmulke and spoke with a heavy Eastern European accent, who had offended my mother. Rugalah cookies and baked apples were acceptable Jewishness, being a practicing Jew was not. Chiam was also one of my parents' first tenants after they bought a four-unit building with money they did not have. (It was at a time when real estate was still affordable in Los Angeles.) Mom fielded phone calls and collected rents and Dad used his MacGuyver-like skills to fix everything under the roof of the four-unit building.

In the beginning, Chiam and my parents were cordial, but as Chiam's list of grievances grew and his Judaica persisted, it was decided on that phone call that it was time for Chiam to go. After all, he was calling at six o'clock at night.

Dad said, "Uh huh, motherfucker. I will be glad to discuss this with you right this fucking minute…" and I tiptoed over to my bedroom door and closed myself behind it. I heard muffled sounds of him calling Chiam a "motherfucker" several more times before slamming the receiver down. I held my breath as Dad's footsteps pounded past my bedroom to his. He opened a drawer and then slammed it shut. His keys jangled as he moved down the hall and out the front door.

Mom yelled after him, "Where are you going?"

My bedroom door stayed closed.

The rest of the evening was quiet, and Dad never returned.

In the morning, I woke with Dad standing over me. "Get up. You're going to learn to paint today." Within the hour, I was at the far end of Chiam's hallway dressed in a small T-shirt and loose-fitting gray sweatpants with a missing drawstring. Every few minutes, the pants would slowly slide down my waist until I had to pull them up.

Chiam's apartment was now empty. There were indentations in the carpet where furniture once stood. There were a few scattered papers strewn about like rolling desert tumbleweeds after a storm had cleared. Dad stood at the other end of the hallway with a paint roller in hand and cigarette between his lips that held together the smirk on his face. He wore a mustard-colored sweatshirt cut off at the shoulders that showed off impressive arms and stretched over his beer gut.

I quietly struggled with my roller, which had a long pole attachment. The roller slid across the wall, and in a few minutes I was covered in a million tiny, cottage-white paint dots. As I watched him, I could not help but think, *that's my dad*. He was imposing and gruff, and he was not covered in paint like I was. He always knew how to be a guy. Something, even now, I had no idea how to be. That's when I first knew, for a fact, I wanted to be just like him. After an hour, Dad and I were in different rooms when curiosity got the better of me. "Hey, Dad," I called, "what happened to Chiam? Did he move away?"

Dad poked his head around the corner and looked at me, sizing me up about how much he should say. I felt a warm rush of guilty fear. My throat began to close and a blubbering started to build in me. It was a time in my life when everything made me want to cry. As he stared at me, I let out a short, audible breath, knowing that I had asked too much. I stood there with my roller dripping paint, curious and frightened.

Dad said, "Chiam did not treat your mother with respect. That's my wife. No one disrespects your mother." He did not elaborate, and no elaboration was needed. I understood.

I felt many things that day, but mostly I felt lightheaded. The 1970s were a time of social chaos and strong, unregulated paint fumes. After a few more hours in Chiam's apartment, Dad took me outside to sit on the lawn. The sitting turned into lying on the lawn, which eventually turned into losing consciousness on the lawn.

I enjoyed chemical side effects. If I were more conscious about my dreams on the lawn, I am sure they would have been about how Dad's scary ways created security. It was not the first time that I was grateful that he had scared the shit out of me. It would also not be the last time.

While I lay there on the lawn, it was the first time I experienced a memorable woozy. I could not have realized that I was more like him in that moment than I ever had been before.

Like many tenants that followed, Chiam sort of drifted away to a place that I learned not to ask questions about. Dad would be there to protect me and Mom, and it was better to stand behind him than in front when he stormed.

***

MY BREATH FLOATED IN the cold air as Dad and I rode along in his bumbling gold Chevy van, off to get a Christmas tree. It was Christmas Eve, and the yearly ritual of last-second tree shopping was an additional thrill, because I was included in what felt like a guy's night. I must have been about eight or nine, and the prospect of doing something with Dad made me feel manly. So manly I felt I would burst into tears at any moment.

Instead, I held it in. One of my uncles asked me if I intended to be a sissy my whole life. They were all tough guys from Chicago, who scowled and ground their teeth at disappointment while walking chest out and head up. They trudged through the world with grit and flicked short-end cigarettes into the middle of the street. They were characters that walked out of a film noir. Dad was their ringleader.

On the other hand, I sniffled and wiped my nose on my sleeve; tears stained my face with regularity. I wept and whined about everything, because everything bothered me to the point of helplessness. If I struck out in Little League to end the game with the bases loaded, which seemed to be every week, forget about it. I crawled under the bed and stayed there to whimper for a couple of hours. In time I learned that men had to suck it up.

That night, I wanted to cry from tears of joy, although the thought that crying was still crying was not lost on me. I sat with Dad in our crappy, two-tone Volkswagen van, bundled in winter clothes. As I looked up at him through the dark, I felt part of the mystical father-and-son relationship I saw on television.

Sensible fathers wore glasses and calmly fixed problems with intellectual prowess. By the end of the episode, there was an understanding that TV-land fathers and sons were a team, part of an unbreakable family bond that held through all of life's challenges. Dad did not wear glasses and did not talk like television fathers. He had a lilting, Midwestern accent, which replaced all of the "o"s with "uh"s.

He wore blue jeans and dark-colored sweatshirts that hid grease stains. His boots had watermarks from working in puddles. Dad was a plumber then, and as I looked at his fists around the steering wheel, I saw the random scrapes and the open wounds of someone who worked with his hands. At each red light, he would smile at me or wink with his blue eyes.

I would find out only later that Mom sent me along with him not for the experience and joy of riding with Dad to buy my first Christmas tree but to insure that he would come back home and stay the night. It had become common for Dad to disappear on Christmas Eve and return on Christmas Day—it would be less likely that there would be a confrontation while I was unwrapping gifts on Jesus's special day.

Dad was smart like that. I was tired but excited as we drove along, the metal tools clanging around behind us in the van.

Dad exited the car with a mission: to get the cheapest tree possible. He stomped through the Douglas fir needles and the pungent scent of pine. Without looking at any of the trees, Dad marched straight up to the unshaven tree maven and said, "What do you have for a buck?" Then Dad took a deep drag from his cigarette.

The tree man responded, "For a dollar, all I have is that brown tree sitting next to the shredder." And the man pointed to a sad tree next to a wood chipper.

"That's not even a fucking tree!" Dad said, and then he looked toward me for an agreement.

The sad tree had started to brown and missed a few key branches in the middle and a lot of needles, but I wanted it anyway. Not because it was nice, but because it was sad. Over the years, I had become accustomed to feeling bad for inanimate objects and began to give them human emotions, usually sadness or loneliness. It seemed unfair to force the sad tree, propped up by the wood chipper, to cozy up with its executioner. I don't know why I created sad trees, lonely stuffed animals, or an unfulfilled plate of past-due grapes, but I felt sorry for everything—hence the incessant blubbering.

"Actually, aren't all these fucking trees heading to the shredder? It's Christmas Eve," Dad said. He picked up a huge, lush green tree and then plopped it back to the ground. "This one is good." Then Dad looked at me. "Did you see that? None of the needles came off. This tree is fresh." He then turned back to the tree man. "How much you got on the two-dollar tree?"

The guy said, "Sorry, I have to get sixteen dollars for the two-dollar tree."

Dad turned around and grabbed me by the shoulder and pulled me toward the car. He climbed back into the car with a moody expression and a long drag on a menthol cigarette. "These fucking guys. Don't they know those fucking things are just going to become mulch in a day or two?" Dad said to the ether more than to me. We skidded out of the lot, leaving the sad tree to its personal plight. There would be other sad trees that night. Dad's annoyance would fade soon enough. There would be more red lights and more father/son bonding. The same scenario would play out a handful of times before someone finally caved to Dad's negotiations and cloud of smoke, which went everywhere he did. It was the thrill of the hunt, as Dad called it, and we returned home with a fat green tree well past my bedtime.

In later years, I grew to understand that Dad's hard negotiations had little to do with trying to get the best tree for the least amount of money possible due to a shortage of cash. It had much more to do with how Dad treated the world. There would be gamesmanship and haggling with grand gestures toward regular working guys who, for the moment, needed to be called "motherfucker" under Dad's breath. He liked stomping around, defiantly flicking cigarette ash onto the floorboard of his car. I think he felt in control. That night I could smell the scent of discount pine and dreamed of my close father-and-son relationship.

Chapter 3

O N THE MORNING I arrived in Spain, I walked through the tall glass doors of my five-star hotel in Sevilla (press trips have their perks) and out into a springtime breeze. I carried a paper map from the concierge and my blue backpack with Dad in it. It was an organic decision to take Dad for a stroll. He had been cooped up in my luggage and I began to feel badly about it, but I did not completely understand why. However, once I slung him over my shoulder and felt his pull against my back, it just felt right. Better than that, I stood taller knowing I carried around my dead father.

Don't mind us, I thought. *It is just me and my dead father out for a stroll. Don't mess with me, or I will swing my dead father over my head and beat you senseless with him.* The idiocy and irony of it all amused me for hours. Secretly, I prayed that curious strangers would ask what was in the backpack.

Together we walked through the fifteenth- and sixteenth-century archways, cathedrals, and plazas and soaked up the sights. I smelled the sugar from the bakery and the freshly brewed coffee. I watched hip Spaniards, who took sips and nibbled as they hurried along crowded streets wearing freshly ironed suits and dresses. All the guys had slicked-back hair and overly worked style—a friend from Madrid would later describe the men as *señoritos*. All the women wore formfitting dresses and aloof expressions. The city was a metrosexual's paradise of parading beautiful people in mysterious dark sunglasses. I turned my head to watch every woman who passed. Every man, too. Every person I saw looked tanned and done up in tailored clothes. I must have appeared homeless.

I brought one carry-on suitcase and a small backpack for Dad. Socks, shirts, and underwear I washed in the sink of my hotel, because I owned no other suitcase and could not justify placing Dad into checked baggage. I also feared that a lack of cabin pressure might make the plastic drum where Dad resided explode in the belly of the airplane. So Dad took up most of the suitcase.

I passed cops and store owners who had character and ponchiness, who appeared to play supporting cast for all the attractive people. They were older. They leaned in doorways, on the many cars parked along the street, or on the long handle of a push broom. They waited on park benches, chatted to each other, and listened to the world at a much slower pace, without a care at all. They acted almost in opposition to the racing of the youth, who pirouetted around them. I pretended some of them eyed me, the stranger and his rucksack, which gave me warm guilty feelings as I doubted Dad had ever seen a place like this. I decided within a few hours that Dad's many lies helped me visit Spain. Briefly, I was grateful.

***

"So, WHY DO YOU think now is the time for opera in Seville?" I said from the second row of a small press conference in a small white room around a long table. It was a lame question. One of many I asked over the hour. I learned early on that much of the question-asking is part of a larger dog-and-pony show.

Dad sat between my feet in my backpack with one of its straps wrapped around my leg, in case anyone burst into the room to rob me. Since Dad didn't fit into the hotel room's safe, I didn't want to leave him in the room. So off to work we went.

The four photographers stood behind us, the seated journalists. Incessantly, they clicked and flashed with big digital single-lens reflex cameras, jockeying for the best camera angle to shoot the producer, a wide, bald guy who wore sunglasses and one of those tan vests with a dozen pockets over a pink dress shirt—a look that said, "I'm in the biz," but just in Spanish.

The event went well. In general, producers want international media to ask lots of questions and help create the illusion of importance. They want photographers to take pictures of gathered media to get buzz. And I sat at the end of the table and wore translation headsets and asked questions and took notes and continued to feel like a fraud. To be fair to my old self, usurping a press trip to scatter Dad's ashes for free was quite a coup. An act I am certain Dad would have appreciated.

I genuinely wanted Spain to get its money's worth. "Over the next five years, how do you see the opera showcase progressing?" I said. The bald producer squirmed in his seat, put a hand to his jaw, and looked up at the ceiling. I sat poised with my pen pressed against my notepad.

"Hopefully, we will keep telling stories that matter, because we are passionate about what we do. We are passionate about life," he said. Then he leaned back in his chair and looked satisfied and certain.

At the end of the day, which had brought similar press events, I took back to the street with Dad. I was in Spain with him draped across my shoulder, not out of love but out of obligation. I was not passionate about what I was doing and not passionate about life. I wanted to tell people that I had not only rescued him from an eternity of being in St. George but that I showed him Spain and made his final wish come true. I held him loosely by the strap as he dangled from one shoulder. I dared any thief in sight to just grab him and run.

Fulfilling his last wish made me feel like I was an idiot. I lied, if only through omission, to Spain, for what? So his wife could feel like the mission was accomplished? His nonsense story about returning home could be validated? If the situation were reversed, I would have sat forever on a shelf. He was a jerk even in death. Maybe I felt like an idiot because part of me still idolized him. And still, there I was, running around with a bag of dirt strapped to my back. We headed unconsciously down to Sevilla's bullfighting ring. The iconic stadium wreaked of old-world-ness with its whitewashed, hand-plastered walls. Instinctively, I bought two tickets from a gold-toothed crone, one for myself and one for Dad, for later that night. I figured I owed Dad a guy's afternoon out and wanted to see the fights, like old times. It was the closest thing I could get to the old Olympic Auditorium, and I needed inspiration.

Dad and I had gone to the Olympic when I was young. Before each visit, I grabbed Dad's arm and dragged him down the hall and into my room. There among the old plates of food and game pieces littered on the floor was an old black-and-white television with tinfoil wrapped around the antenna. I pointed at the television as the Los Angeles Thunderbirds skated or Victor Rivera and the Twin Devils wrestled or Danny "Little Red" Lopez punched. I looked up at Dad, still holding his arm, and hoped his excitement matched my own. His approval, at the time, was all I ever wanted. He feigned enough interest for occasional tickets.

The Olympic was an icon for blue-collar entertainment in Los Angeles in the 1970s and aired boxing, wrestling, and roller derby on the old UHF channel fifty-two. The building was falling apart, dingy, noisy, and had a slimy layer of grease, peanut shells, fake popcorn butter, and beer covering the floors and seats. Crowds rarely filled the place, but the audiences made up for it with loudness. Dad and I were surrounded by the cheering in Spanish and broken English from the downtown Angelenos. Beer splashed across us as wax-paper cups were thrown at the ring, and fights broke out in the rows behind us. Fights broke out in front of us. Fights broke out in the ring and on the track. That was our guy's night out, which was more important than the results of the bouts.

I knew most of the outcomes were prearranged but hoped I was wrong. Not that it mattered. Dad leaned back and swirled his cerveza against the ridiculousness of it all and kept me well stocked with peanuts. He never cared for sports the way I did, but I felt him stare down at me, watching me engrossed in every moment. When there was a break in the action, I would look up at him just to see if he was paying attention to the games. He was not. He was always just watching me. He occasionally wiped a beer-foam mustache across my upper lip.

The last time we visited the Olympic I was sixteen. I had seen an ad that wrestling was returning there after a several-year hiatus. We arrived ten minutes before the start and got first-row seats. The room was cavernous and populated by a few families with a few kids chasing each other around the ring.

By the time the show started, there were fifty people in the theater built to hold thousands. The ring was lit up with spotlights, and I was giddy again with the nostalgia of hanging around with Dad. The bags under his eyes were heavier, his face more worn, but he was still my dad.

The main event consisted of four bodybuilders and fourteen fat guys who made up the battle royale, where eighteen men slammed into each other over the vague ideal of good-versus-evil supremacy and one ultimate victor. At one point, one of the wrestlers was watching alongside of us. The guy was huge, rippling muscles, veins popping out of his arms and neck, covered in intimidating tattoos, wore a Mohawk, and he stood there with Dad.

Dad struck up a conversation with him. "So why aren't you in there? Aren't you supposed to kick ass or something?"

"For this crowd?" the wrestler said, waving a hand to shoo away the idea. Dad then threw his arm around the guy like he had known him for ages and even tried to get him in a headlock. They both laughed. I shuddered and took a step back. If I remember correctly, the wrestler's schtick was bending a steel bar around his head. After they separated, Dad poked his new brawny friend in the chest like old wrestling interviews. I thought the guy was going to throw Dad in the ring and kill him. Instead they talked, without me, until after the light went back on in the auditorium and the final bits of the tiny crowd went home.

***

WITH A FEW HOURS to kill and bullfighting tickets in my pocket, I took Dad out on the town. He sat on the café table while I sipped an espresso outside in the sun. "So what do you think?" I said quietly to my backpack with Dad in it. "So this is it. You're in Spain, you fucking jerk."

While he was alive, I think I swore at him once. Now that he was dead, I granted myself the privilege with abandon. The oddness of talking to the sack would grate at me and felt embarrassing, but I wanted this trip to be memorable for him. As I leaned back and sipped, I described the black-veiled religious ladies with their lacy hoop skirts, weathered cigar-smoking men playing chess in the park, youthful hipster couples holding hands, and other charming clichés that embodied southern Spain. I would eventually learn to embrace our one-sided chats, but in the beginning, I felt phony and manipulated. I was carrying on a charade for my own benefit, although there seemed to be a purpose to all the talking and description. A deep part of me wanted to make up for lost time. I spent the next hour trying to create a world where I spoke and Dad listened.

✳✳✳

As I CAME THROUGH the tunnel, I saw the bright white chalk lines and orange clay of the bullfighting ring. The roar of the crowd, while in Spanish, swept through me in a familiar way. With beer and peanuts in hand, I sat down on the bleacher and placed a beer on Dad's seat, pretended it was his ashes. I decided to make beer a symbol of Dad's presence. Over time, I became more comfortable replacing Dad with symbols, and so talked to the beer just like I would have talked to the plastic container. Without the conspicuous plastic jug, I became more at ease. The conversation felt more like a prayer.

As I looked around, I saw women with floppy sun hats and gold-clasped clutch bags, T-shirted men who read the newspaper and smoked cigars, and moony-eyed couples holding hands all pressed together in the sun, leaving no seat unfilled, to watch death. The rumble of voices anticipating the match hit me in my gut. I leaned forward with my hands on my knees and Dad at my side. A hush fell over the stadium and the bull burst into the arena kicking up dirt and looking for something to attack.

I leaned over and whispered to the full beer and empty seat. "Okay, so there is this bull and he is huge. He's sort of a dingy white and blowing some major snot bubbles." Regardless of illusory

David-versus-Goliath appearances, the bull was already dead, in my estimation.

The bull ran around the ring to the sounds of cheering. Ladies waved their hats and some fans stood and clapped, others yelled and hooted. Confused, the bull charged one direction and then another.

Then, satin-clad matador's helpers, called picadors, methodically goaded the bull to charge and run around the arena more. "Okay, Dad, these guys just ran up behind the bull and stabbed it with frilly spears. And now we have blood," I said. Once its juices got flowing, the bull was attacked relentlessly for twenty minutes by the picadors, and later by guys on armored and blindfolded horses. All the while, cheers filled the arena. It's got to blow being the bull.

Then the matador entered the arena, charming and cool, knowing, I assumed, that the bull had a weakness—and that he had a team of professionals watching his back. The matador waved to the crowd, which roared its approval. He wore a funny black hat, a pink embroidered bolero jacket, and matching spangled culottes. He was armed with a sword thin enough to pit olives and sharp enough to slice paper.

"Okay, there is a teeny man waving a cape around."

"Shhh," the man in front of me said, before turning back around and settling into the fight. I thought, *Fuck you, jackass,* but lowered my voice and continued.

"The teeny man is just standing there while the giant bull just runs circles around him." Then a spontaneous chorus of boos erupted from the arena that shook our seats. "The crowd is booing the teeny man. I have no idea why. The teeny man just stuck another feathery spear into the side of the bull. Lots of snot bubbles and blood," I whispered.

I wanted to see the bullfights for Dad, but also for the cultural experience. It was true. Spain had made a spectator sport of killing a huge animal by inviting fearless, or stupid, skinny men in Capri pants and a thick coat of machismo into a pen with the bull.

The sun dipped below the stadium and cast a shadow across our seats, and I felt a chill. After a few minutes, the bull, streaked with blood along its back and shoulders, had been slowed and hypnotized into submission. As the picadors kept the bull busy, the matador ceremonially retrieved a long, shining sword wrapped in silks and goose-stepped back toward the hapless bull.

The crowd bellowed and murmured as the inevitable became obvious. After a few more olés and waves of the cape, the matador would bury the sword deep between the bull's shoulder blades. When done correctly, the bull would drop like a sack of potatoes.

The bull slowed, almost mesmerized by the constant action and perhaps frustrated by chasing the shadowy ghost of the maroon bedspread. It was shocking how quickly the bull tired. He moved from ferocious to confused to docile within a few minutes. I wondered if the bull ever knew that its life was on the line.

Unfortunately for bulls, fortitude is a human quality. I imagined, hopefully, throughout my day with Dad at the bullfights that the bull would fight and flail around until the bitter end, or that the bull would win one or two of the matches even, the matador carried out on a gurney, but that was not the way it worked. With the bull bleeding, ragged, and backed up against the wooden fence, he appeared to be saying in his final moments, "I give up. Kill me now." And, finally, after running the bull in panting circles after his silky, flashing cape, the matador pulled out the blade. "Olé!" the arena cried. The bull gave in to exhaustion. Only then did the matador plunge the blade.

"Dad," I said. "This first bull is toast."

Sadly, the first matador was a yutz, who stabbed and missed the fast-kill spot on the bull's back several times. The crowd erupted and booed with a venom I thought reserved for the Olympic. The bull lolled its head from side to side and briefly looked like Janet Leigh to the matador's Anthony Perkins.

"Just like tapas and Flamenco," I told Dad, "this is as close as we are going to get to roller derby, boxing, and wrestling in Spain."

I wanted to walk away from my first bullfight with moral superiority that such barbarism could never appeal to me, that it was beneath my curiosity. However, I treated life as if I were always walking down a dark alley. So much time had been spent sizing up everyone around me and knowing that everyone had a weakness that could be exposed. The idea was frightening, liberating, and exciting.

I watched from the edge of my bench and took turns admiring the wild crowd's judgment and the bull's vanquished adrenaline. I wanted to take pity on its plight, but I didn't. I craved seeing its death. It was a morbid realization, but I wanted to see something larger than life that showed power beyond measure get reduced to a lifeless heap. I wanted to see evidence of what I intuitively knew: that life in any form is fragile.

"Dad, this is horrible, but I can't stop watching."

Toward the end of the first match, when the matador finally found the bull's off switch and the bull's carcass was eventually dragged away, I imagined Dad must have had his own final moment that felt like the bull. He lay in front of the television in his tattered boxers, smoking down yet another cigarette next to a billowing ashtray after having been jabbed one too many times during his life, thinking, *Okay, kill me now.* And the Universe said, "Gotcha."

***

After the start of the second slaying, I admitted to Dad, "So I don't know what the hell is going on." An English-speaking Spaniard named Mario, who sat a few seats away, began to bend my ear about the nuanced points of bullfighting and the national pride felt "by every Spaniard" about it. He wore a wide-brimmed hat and chain-smoked brown cigarillos in a way that made those around him slide away. His wrinkled button-down shirt stretched, leaving pale gaps of stomach that would make sensible people pray for zippered clothing. We spoke in turns over a beleaguered young couple who sat between us until he bulled his way into the seat closest to me—sandwiching me between his cigarillos and Dad's beer—and pushed the young couple to the other side of him.

He explained, "Ah yes, footwork, concentration, and stillness, this shows the true heart of a warrior." I cozied up to his nicotine cloud. The matador hopped as the two-thousand-pound brown bull ran a tight circle around him, and Mario jumped out of his seat.

"Oh, did you see that? Appalling," he said as he pointed toward the ring, and jeers filled the arena. "Such a tragedy. He is too frightened." Then he waved his arm toward the ring with disgust. "Ach, you have to wait to see a real matador, one that has experience and finesse."

He kept talking about feet positions and posture, and I faded away to liberate peanuts from their shells. I scanned the seats around me, watching all the portly men with opinions about the match. I finally said, "But isn't the bull just going to die at the end?"

Mario flung his arms out wide and said, "Of course. It is too easy to kill this thing. There is always more perfection and more to discuss."

As dead bulls piled up and the sun sank lower on the horizon, Mario continued to educate me on the bullfights. In between the action, I told Mario about Dad, Cádiz, "Ave Maria," and the roller derby. The bullfight replayed itself several more times, always punctuated with the sharp end of a long sword.

I sat depressed as Mario lectured on, and the rise and fall of the cheers and boos moved without cease. My malaise broke when the man on the other side of Dad tried to move the beer to the ground, and I watched as foam slid over the brim of the paper cup and down its sides.

The arena was hot and crowded. People wanted to stretch out, but I didn't care. I told him, *"Mi padre es muerto, pero quiere cervasa."*

Dad is dead, but still wants beer.

I said it with a half smile to calm any frayed nerves, but I had already decided to punch him in the mouth and get arrested. The Spaniard was thin, well-dressed, had thick dark hair and sunglasses, and sat next to his pretty girlfriend. He waved his hands at me, as if to say, "Come on, put your drink on the floor so I can have a few extra inches of space."

I put the beer back on the bench. It was the space I had paid for and that was Dad's spot. I stood up with vinegar in my veins and I flexed my boney arms. The prospect of getting thrown into jail on Dad's behalf, defending his seat, would have been the honorable thing to do. The slender and stylish man looked at me as if I were a nut. I remember thinking that if Dad's ashes were there, I would have beat the guy with them. I could almost see the gray cloud of Dad floating over our seats as his jug broke open.

Then Mario stood up and put his hand on my shoulder. "I think we should enjoy the bullfights again." I turned to Mario, saw his kind face. The anger in me died quickly and I sat down.

Dad was proud. I could feel it. So I sat there with Mario and Dad on uncomfortable benches and watched a little more death until the sun fell behind the arena and everything felt colder.

I left before the last match and thanked Mario. I could not just leave the beer representing Dad sitting in the sun and so I carried him through the aisle and up the stairs, my back to the arena as the next bull stormed into it.

After several years of sobriety, I was not going to drink the beer, regardless of the obvious poetry. Then, it crossed my mind to dump it in the garbage can, which might have been poetic on another level. Instead, I slowly poured the beer in a thirsty, oversized plant just outside the arena.

Just as I wanted more from the bull, I wanted more from my father's final moments than to be filled with fighting and flailing. The reality is Dad had died alone in a crappy mobile home in a crappy trailer park in a crappy town. It was a far cry from what I had hoped or expected of him. In both cases, the deaths of the bulls and Dad were sad but predictable. It gnawed at me in a distant way.

I did not want to think about Dad and watch a bull get slaughtered at the same time. The two had too much in common. I wanted to remember Dad only as a badass.

***

SHEER, STRIPED-PRINT CURTAINS HUNG from cheap white rods and blew softly in the April breeze. Dad and I lay on our bellies watching Vin Scully, the voice of Dodgers baseball, while eating from a tray of Ritz crackers and a jar of Skippy peanut butter on the bed in my parents' bedroom. I was thirteen, and the Dodgers were playing the Chicago Cubs.

Although the Cubs were in last place, for one summer, we never missed a televised game. Dad wasn't much of a fan, but he never let an opportunity to reminisce about his days growing up in Chicago slide by. The stories had a similar thread: elaborations about arguments on train cars, Golden Gloves competitions, and walking down the wrong street late at night. Every story he told offered a moral of how to defend what he called a "life of integrity."

This day he would tell me about how he ran into and eventually arm-wrestled Ernie "Mr. Cub" Banks for twenty bucks. I remember how he described things with enthusiastic hand gestures, biceps flexing, and a mock demonstration of the event, which knocked over the jar of peanut butter, sending the butter knife across the room before landing in an open drawer of rolled socks. Even though he lost to Ernie, Dad remained my hero. He began to spin another tale about Chicago when he abruptly stopped and pointed at the window and its billowing curtain. Along with the flowing curtains was an arm reaching inside the window. It took a moment before I realized what was wrong. My heart leaped into my throat. The next thing I saw was my father, carefully and calmly sidling near the window. As Dad grabbed the arm, the scent of peanut butter filled the room, and I thought how much louder struggles are in the movies. I was equally amazed and scared. It seemed graceful as my father pulled the arm farther through the window with one hand as the other hand reached toward an old hatchet he kept in the top dresser drawer for situations like this.

Dad made a point of showing me all of the locations throughout the house where he had hidden weapons. When I was younger, he pulled an eighteen-inch pipe from between the cushions of the couch, one end carefully wrapped in silver duct tape for a better grip. "Remember, step into it when you swing this at someone, just like in baseball." He stepped toward me, swinging the pipe at my ribs, stopping short of hitting me. "Go straight to the head, but the ribs are an easy target, and it is good because it sets up the second shot," he told me. This time he backhanded the pipe toward my face, again stopping before carefully pressing the cold metal against my temple, jaw, the bridge of my nose, and neck—showing me the key strike points to get my important ideas across. "Remember, don't be a fucking pussy. It's just like baseball."

He went on to explain that he preferred heavy, blunt objects for outer rooms of a house: bats in the living room, pipes in the dining room, that sort of thing. He reasoned that blunt instruments were good for breaking bones and teeth, for negotiation without permanent injury, which might lead toward a road of rehabilitation. "Everyone deserves a second chance," he said. However, break-ins through a bedroom window required a devious mind looking for an element of surprise on a sleeping or disabled victim, an act less worthy of forgiveness. Slicing-type weapons, he explained, were good for ending things quickly. He always told me, "Just make sure the cops understood you felt your life was in danger."

The arm belonged to a young man, maybe in his early twenties, wearing a red-and-black football jersey, who was struggling against being pulled farther into our home. Dad's fingers strained toward the hatchet, which was just out of his reach.

"Don't just fucking sit there, give me a hand."

I scrambled out of bed toward the dresser, knocking over the tray of Ritz crackers with a crash. I wanted to close my eyes and pray this would go away.

"What the fuck is wrong with you?" Dad grunted.

I picked up the hatchet with both hands and hesitated with it. It was dark brown cold metal with a worn wooden handle and heavier than it appeared. Outside, there was a loud bang. A second young man was now pulling the first back out the window. Dad tried to grab him with his other free hand but missed. The two men took off running and Dad leaned out window to get a better view of the thieves. He turned for his car keys, grabbed a handful of my hair, and pushed me down the hall and out the front door. The thieves were running down the street as we hopped into Dad's gold Chevy van, the kind with the bubble window in the back, and raced after them.

My hands gripped tightly around the hatchet. I tried not thinking about what might happen. Still, I imagined having to swing the hatchet full force at one of the guys. In my mind, I saw blood spatter and Dad egging me on to do it again.

We skidded to a stop in front of Mr. Roberts' house as they ran up the driveway. "Those fucking morons are trapped," Dad said, smirking, and he reached behind the driver's side seat, pulling out a monkey wrench. I knew he was right. The Roberts' had tall fences in their yard. He looked at me and then calmly said, "Don't be a pussy, all right? Be a man and defend your fucking home."

We both got out of the car and walked up the driveway. Dad held the monkey wrench in one hand with its head resting on the top of his shoulder. We then walked past Mr. Roberts' guava tree. On more restful afternoons, Dad and I would occasionally stop by and feast on overripe guava that had fallen in the grass. The two were trying to scale a tall black sheet-metal fence in the Roberts' yard. When they saw us, the one wearing the blue zipper-front hooded sweatshirt turned and charged toward us. His jeans were cuffed and his hands were clawed, which did make sense to me, but I still didn't know how to defend it. His tennis shoes slipped slightly on the wet grass just as he got to my father. He seemed to move in slow motion. I knew I had enough time to get a good swing at him, but my arms felt like Jell-O, my legs buried in cement.

Dad brought the wrench off his shoulder and down across the guy's temple. The sound was full, much bigger than I had expected. The bones broke simultaneously throughout the entire side of his face. His body went limp before falling backward in the same way old football clips showed opposing players driven into the ground by Dick Butkus. The guy lay on his back in an unnatural position in the damp grass, and the whites of his eyes bulged through his closed eyelids in a way I had never seen before.

The guy with the red-and-black jersey looked much younger than he did when he was dangling in my parents' bedroom window. He began to sob. "I'm sorry. We are poor. I promise never to bother you again. I know nothing. Please, please leave me alone."

I knew he was telling the truth and felt badly for him. Dad paused for a moment and then gestured, as if to usher him past us and down Mr. Roberts' driveway. With great hesitation, he started for the driveway. When he got in front of me, Dad yelled, "Be a man and fucking crack this guy. Do it now!" Without thinking, I raised up the hatchet with both hands. The young man covered his face with his hands.

"Dad, I can't do this. I really want to, but he said he was sorry—and I don't know if I could do it anyway." There was another pause, then Dad stepped forward and came up with the wrench, catching the first guy underneath the chin, snapping his head back and spraying blood across my Los Angeles Dodgers Home Field T-shirt, before he hit the ground.

Dad turned toward me in disgust and nodded at his van. Halfway down the driveway, he put his arm around me. Neither one of us looked back. Dad methodically buckled up for the half-block ride home. I knew what had happened was wrong. Still, I rarely thought about those men—boys, really—again. Dad had a strong code of ethics about taking care of the family, because no one else would.

There had to be a penalty when we were crossed. There had to be a reaction.

"Don't worry, they won't be back. I think they learned something today. Everyone deserves a second chance." He swiveled, turning around in the driver's seat before sliding the monkey wrench back in its usual place, and then turned the ignition. As we pulled in front of our house, I felt older. He smiled at me and said, "You can let go of the hatchet now." He was still my hero.

✳✳✳

AFTER I PUT DOWN the hatchet, Dad and I started drifting apart. The drift was both cosmic and practical. From the practical side, I had solid reason to take shelter from Dad's life lessons. He was nuts. I still appreciated Dad's manliness, unpredictability, and the obvious respect he received, but I was growing up. The next four years passed quickly and had become like a video game. With each new level, everything moved faster, less time to react, more room for error, so much to explore.

I spent most of my free time playing the Atari 2600 Tank Battle game against the computer, holed up in my room surrounded by half-eaten plates of food. My grades nosedived. I felt insecure and awkward. My face turned red and erupted in zits. The process was primal. I had questions, but I did not know what they were. I would not have asked even if I knew. I lived in a house without discussion. Communication revolved around basic questions about survival or the acceptance of a demand.

"Is Dad home?" I asked my mother.

"No," she said.

"Is there anything for dinner?"

"It is in the pot from last night. Get it yourself."

I was un-uniquely miserable and alone.

I began to steal and snoop during the summer before middle school. I crouched on the cold tile counter in the kitchen when no one was home. The small brown bottles were lined up on the second shelf next to the chocolate Ex-Lax bar. I took one pill from every brown container and broke off five squares of the Ex-Lax, which tasted good in the beginning yet was problematic later. I snuck the pills into my room. This was not a conscious effort on my part to learn what any of the pills did. I just knew that they were supposed to do something, and I wanted something different. I woke up dazed, and then I sat on the toilet for an hour. This was no deterrent.

A week later, I found myself in the living room closet. It was a dark vacuum of curious debris. It had historically become the hiding place for my Christmas presents and anything else that could be described as miscellaneous. In it I found on the floor a 1970s *Playboy* magazine and a fancy bottle of Drambuie liqueur.

Within the year, I routinely disappeared to sneak pills, smoke cigarettes, think about women, and seek out more porn when the closet *Playboy* became too familiar. I discovered a Dorothy Stratton *Playboy* in a nearby sewer, which was better than finding money. Damp filth slathered across it. I lay in the gutter and stretched my arm deep into the sewer's grate, but I couldn't reach it. The habit of searching alleys and sewers for free things extended the thrill of stealing and getting something for nothing. I struggled with Dorothy's manhole cover and finally pried it up with a small crowbar I had stolen from my father. I muscled the manhole cover over far enough to fit into the sewer. Thick, rotting goo covered the magazine, but I decided after all the work to get it, I had to keep it, and took it home with a sense of accomplishment. I threw it in the ivy-covered walkway between my room and a fence billowing with vines for later use. When the clumped pages of Dorothy stopped working, I began to steal porn from several of the local mini-markets, not to mention cigarettes and pills.

In time, I added gambling into my every day, starting with the Rossmore shuttle bus to Hollywood Park, where I gave the tall, delinquent kids money to bet on the horses when I should have been in English class. I imagine this was my attempt to find a kind of adolescent independence and something to quell an almost constant feeling of fear. My new hobbies fueled another reason not to see Dad: I didn't want to get caught.

By the time I was fifteen, I had built a complicated, satisfying, secret life.

I crawled under the bed, tore a hole in the bottom of the box spring, and filled it with my personal contraband: stray cigarettes, a cheap Bic lighter, a few cans of Budweiser, a pack of Zig-Zags, a bud or two of cheap dope, a travel-sized mouthwash, cough drops, and several toilet paper squares wrapped around a small cache of blue Valiums, white Vicodin, and a few highly prized Quaaludes— my favorites.

The porn was harder to hide because under the mattress was simply too cliché. I eventually pulled up the carpeting in my closet, threw the stash of porn under the unstapled corner, and piled my junk on top. The Dorothy Stratton issue started to stink from soaking in the gutter water and so I pushed her out under my bedroom window screen into the ivy-strewn side of the house, to eventually be eaten by rats. The bottle of Drambuie was slowly sipped away and refilled with olive oil—as if no one would notice—and then carefully thrown away in Dorothy's sewer when I felt certain the bottle that hid in the back of the closet had been forgotten.

I was ashamed of my behavior but held on to the distant sense that I was learning to be just like Dad. The secrecy I cultivated created a push-pull, love-hate relationship with him. I kept the same distance from my own friends for fear of getting caught and perhaps honing my skills for seclusion. It all felt normal.

While I avoided Dad, I no longer had the same fear of him. I learned to talk around questions, helped him when he wanted, and appeared busy the rest of the time. And I was busy. Dishonesty is a full-time job. I had too much invested in hiding my noble quest for glossy women and altered states to pay attention to anything else.

It was a lifestyle that would work its way into most everything I did for the next fifteen years.

Around the same time, another important thing happened: my parents' wise investment made money. That entire time Dad had spent fixing, painting, scraping, and scrubbing began to pay off. We, as a family, were no longer constantly broke.

"What are you going to do with it?" Dad said with a wry grin as he pulled out a crumpled ten and handed it to me.

"I dunno," I said. "Go out and do something. I guess."

Then he would clap me on the back as I wandered away.

I think his generosity gave him great pleasure and pride, knowing he didn't have to scramble for rent. Dad was now able to throw his son a few bucks here and there.

And I needed more dough for gas and pills.

She left her blue VW bug parked diagonally against the curb with the car door open and the lights on. It was our moment. She and I climbed through the back doors into my inherited Chevy van, which had uncomfortable, thick shag carpeting throughout and mock-wood paneling on the sides. I had hidden three-quarters of a mayonnaise jar's worth of Southern Comfort and a pack of Djarum clove cigarettes in my mobile lair. I frequently kept a stash of bad weed and Valiums around, too. For some reason, the alcohol felt so much more acceptable than the pills, which were a private, anytime oasis. I was in high school and considered myself a romantic. The van was equipped with a stove and refrigerator. Neither worked, but I kept a couple of lavender-scented votive candles and a handful of strike-anywhere matches in the refrigerator for mood lighting. These were never used.

I closed the doors to leave the quiet street behind us.

She had long, dark hair and light eyes and wore a jean jacket and tucked her pants into her boots. I unscrewed the mayonnaise jar. She took small sips. I took large ones. The booze was warm and curdling from being buried in a flap of heavy shag, or from mixing with Miracle Whip residue. The scent of lasting love hung heavy in the air, and her kisses tasted like receptive panic. We unbuttoned, unzipped, and un-elasticized each other in the darkness of my rolling fantasy suite.

As sweet nothings were exchanged I saw my mother's distorted face in the bubble window on the side of the van. Then she banged on the sliding side door of the van. Thud, thud, thud. "Devin, are you in there? Your father wants to speak to you this instant!"

I waited for a moment in confusion before I said, "I'm busy." My female party guest looked at me like, "It's time to stop now." While I understood the logic, I did not stop. In the weight of the moment, I felt my face heat up from embarrassment and I became uncomfortably self-aware, but I would be damned if I stopped. I had to save face with my muse squirming beneath me.

Mom moved away from the bubbled window and said, "Your father is waiting."

"Yeah, I really don't care right now. I will come up shortly." I felt increasingly sick and horrified.

"Your father…" Mom started to continue.

I interrupted and said, "Would you get the hell out of here?"

With that, Mom left; at least I hoped she left. I made a particular point not to look toward the bubble window in the back of the van. I felt better when I heard her slippers slide against the concrete and become more distant as she shuffled away. I took a few extra minutes with my lady friend and bid a fond adieu to romance. I watched her blue bug pull away into the darkness.

When I got upstairs, Mom stood in a floral print nightgown with her arms folded across her chest. Dad stared at the floor in his boxers, smoking a cigarette, sitting at the dining room table. Both looked weary, their hair flung in contorted sleep positions.

I reeked of clove cigarettes and soured Southern Comfort. I was annoyed that my sex life had been temporarily derailed, but I prepared to be grilled and busted in a multitude of ways and was not up for all the lying.

"Your father is so angry with you. You kept him up all night," Mom said. She waved her hand to express herself. "Do you know what it looked like from up here? It looked like terrorists had taken you. Couldn't she park a fucking car, that slut? Who is she, that slut?" Mom looked at Dad. Dad did not look up from the floor. Instead he took a slow, cool drag, never raising his head, and let the smoke envelop his face. "Your father was very nervous. He was waiting for the police to come." She clamored on and on. I lost track of what she was saying. I was red in the face and found myself rocking back and forth, embarrassed but angry, squeezing my lips together, afraid of what I would say. While it was completely my fault, I felt indignant.

Dad interrupted and said, "Enough already." He raised his head and looked at Mom. "It's time for you to go." His face drooped from age and exhaustion. His eyes were bloodshot, his big belly jutted out. "I need to talk to my son."

Mom folded her arms across her chest again. "Okay, go on," she said.

"I will, without you. Now go to sleep."

Mom hesitated and slowly turned around and left the room.

Dad held up his index finger as if to say "hold on a minute" and waited for the bedroom door to open and close. Then he turned his ear toward the hallway and waited to listen for any stirrings. While Dad waited, I wondered how I should approach this. Whatever it was going to be would have nothing to do with the truth. I stank of cheap booze, cigarettes, and lady musk. While this was not new, it was the first time I had been caught, and in such a stupid way.

Dad said in a low, quiet voice, "So listen, wait!" Then he held up an index finger and listened intently for Mom. When he was certain, he stood up and slammed his foot down on the floor with a bang that reverberated through the house. He yelled, "You will never speak that way to me or your mother again. Do you fucking understand me?" Then he waited with his index finger up.

Confused, I started, "But I haven't said…"

Dad continued, "You don't fucking get it. There are rules in this fucking house." Then he paused again with a finger up, rigid in the air.

Still confused. "Okay, Dad…"

"Who the fuck do you think you are?" Dad stomped on the floor loudly and waited. Then, "I don't give a shit. Give me your car keys." And waited. I reached into my pocket and started to pull them out with a jangle.

Annoyed, he looked at me as if to say, "put those away," and bellowed, "Not another word!" Then he sat down and smashed his cigarette out in the ashtray. He pulled out another from a green pack and lit it. He exhaled fully, sank into the upholstered chair, and lowered his voice to a whisper. "Okay, we are going to have to come up with a plan B. While you're grounded, you're going to find a new study partner. Let's call him Jeremy. He'll need some help with homework from you. Math. You're good at math."

For me, the picture was coming into view. I was not going to have to lie about anything. I was not going to have to explain anything. A small nugget of relief grew inside of me. I was going to be allowed my independence. I would keep my car and now had a reason to get out of everything. My body convulsed as anxiety turned into giddy relief. The chill stayed in my bones for another half an hour, and I would shudder every few minutes.

Dad leaned in and softly said, "Go live your life, but be careful." Then he leaned back in his chair and took another deep breath, as if distracted by something. "For fuck's sake, your mother sure talks a lot." He took another drag from his cigarette and snapped back into the moment. "Okay, apologize first thing. Tell her how really rotten I am, and then make plans with Jeremy," he said. "And would you wash your fucking hands?"

For me the clouds parted. I discovered that with a little planning and dishonesty, I could please everyone. It was an idea that I understood through osmosis, but Dad's coaching gave me a warm glow.

In the morning, I apologized to Mom with my chin held high. I felt the best connection to Dad I had felt in ages. For a moment, I was one of the boys. It was a good feeling, which would not last long.

During my apology, Mom interrupted and called me a Nazi with her arms folded across her chest and her long hair in a disorganized mass on top of her head. The use of "Nazi" was Mom's most loathsome of critiques, which almost made me sing. She was still fuming at my disrespect, and it was all I could do not to grin. I had been given the go-ahead to manipulate the world. I told her about math tutoring and I waited to see if she would buy it or ask any questions.

It was then I understood Dad was never mad at me, really. He expressed anger on my behalf. When I was scared or crying, he showed anger. Not at me, but for me. When I could not stand up for myself, his anger did. He showed me what men did. I think I learned to understand him more. Of course, this took years to piece together. He got mad at the situation, maybe the injustice. He was still the one who gave me long hugs and would pull me into to a tight squeeze while the two of us lay in bed to watch a game. He was the one who loved me or showed tenderness, but this soon waned.

It was not that he was less loving, he became more detached. I had too. My drinking and using was in full swing, and Vegas comped cigarettes and beer.

I had become good at waiting. I knew how to grind out a win over time, not only with poker but with life—or so I thought. I was able to sneak through the window of opportunity and grab what I could and sneak back out before it slid shut. It felt like a spiritual transcendence as I became more like Dad.

***

WHEN I WAS A teenager, Dad began to drink less often but with more ferocity, or maybe I learned to recognize the stumbling and slurred speech more easily. His eyes were glassy, his breath pungent. He came home with clenched fists and a mouth full of provocation. The conversations, regardless of how innocently they started, became arguments.

Growing up, I swore that I would never drink or smoke. I had already seen enough to know better. At the same time, when I was twelve, I stole two packs of Dad's Salem regulars and two cans of Budweiser on a crowded Thanksgiving and snuck around to our smallish yard that Dad had taught me to fight in. It was sort of a no-man's-land. No one ever went back there. I smoked and drank like I was in a race—until I barfed into the ivy. My first thought was that I was not doing it right.

Within a couple of years, I had become quite proficient at stocking, hiding, and obtaining what I wanted. I had to put distance between myself and those of the living world. There was always a homeless guy or liquor store that would not care how old I was for booze and cigarettes. I found most of the pills in the medicine cabinets of the parents of my friends. It was the eighties, and most adults I knew had a decent supply of Valium and Vicodin on hand. Luckier days produced Quaaludes or Seconal. My parents also kept a fair number of downers in the medicine cabinets. Sometimes a few stray painkillers laid on the coffee table or on the top of my parents' dresser in their bedroom, or a lone, sticky pill could be found at the bottom of my mother's purse, tacked to an unwrapped piece of gum. I also discovered hash and pot—treats that usually required additional planning.

It was a time when my whole face throbbed from red, puss-filled zits—a justification to hide out in its own right. I normally locked myself in my room when I was home and high. The room was a mess, but cozy, so I could lightly play guitar to myself while I reclined on my bed.

Dad banged on the door before opening it. He stuck his head tightly between the door and the doorjamb as he opened it a crack. His face was puckered with a cigarette between his lips, his eyes were wide, swimming, and red. Without removing the cigarette, he joked, "Your father wants to have a serious conversation with you," his native Chicago accent overly pronounced from daytime drinking. Under normal circumstances, I could temporarily talk my way out of the dialogue and then deal with the consequences later. I would say something like, "I am going to sleep and then I have some homework." Or "I will be out in a minute," followed by "I love you," and within a few minutes he would just forget about it.

I said, "I have work to do and I twisted my ankle. I have to keep it off the ground. I also think I ate some bad fish sticks at lunch. I don't feel so good."

Dad just stood there. "Who are you shitting?" he said. "I am not leaving until you get your ass up and talk to your father." He jutted his lower lip, pushing the cigarette straight up and against his nose. Smoke drifted into his eyes and he narrowed them at me. I could see the playful glow in his eyes turn salty. "I guess your father is just going to stand here and wait for his son to talk to his father," he said.

Knowing I had little choice, I slid the guitar off of my chest and slowly stretched. I let out an audible grunt intended to let him know that I was producing great effort to deal with him. I thought about how high I was. How obvious was it? How high was he? How oblivious was my being high to someone as high as he was? Then I started thinking about eating a sandwich. It did not matter what kind. I also wanted marshmallows. I knew there was nothing in the kitchen, but I thought I would go look anyway. I sat myself up and wobbled toward my bedroom door. There was Dad's face, still smoking in the crack in the door. How did he get there? I had taken a couple Valium after eating a pot brownie. I had no idea how long I'd been standing there looking at him. I decided to play it cool and pulled the door open and walked passed him down the hall.

He followed me.

"So what do you want?" I said as I walked into the dining room.

"Who the fuck are you copping an attitude with?"

I turned to face him as we hit the dining room. I was sick of him. He was a bully I was tired of having to avoid. I wanted marshmallows, and not to be followed from room to room. I put my hands on my hips and took a deep breath. "What?" I said, avoiding eye contact because I did not know what state my pupils were in.

As I stood there, I noticed I was looking down at Dad. Not metaphorically, but literally. I was hitting a long-awaited high school growth spurt and he was shrinking. He was still much wider, thicker, and stronger, but I had convinced myself over the next few quiet seconds that my new height advantage, about an inch, was now significant. I also noticed that my arms were longer than his. I had the reach. I had stoned-man's advantage. I did not stop to consider that I knew nothing about boxing or wrestling, and everything I knew about street fighting I learned from him and he fought really dirty. I also did not take into account that I now had a couple of Valiums coursing through my veins and marijuana in my stomach. It did not matter. That moment, in my mind, was seminal. It was a time for me to stand up to the old man and gain some self-respect. A mythological time when the son becomes the top dog and the father goes out to pasture and learns his place—I no longer wore pantaloons and a macramé sweater vest.

I leaned forward and lunged at him, pushing him back into the wall and knocking a large painting in the dining room askew. For a nanosecond, I felt a physical surge. I felt powerful as I pinned Dad against the wall, but the moment did not last. He laughed in my face. It was a noxious blast that stunk of salami, American cheese, and cigarettes. My brief confidence left me. I suppose I had time to apologize, but my ego was not ready to give up. I tried to press his arms down to control him. Dad had construction worker strength. He lifted his arm and I went with it. He spun me around several times, pushing and slapping me around some, although nothing would be bruised except my pride.

All the flailing and flexing of my baby-girl arms were for naught. Everything failed, and with every worthless move, I felt more belittled and humiliated. The only thing that worked was triggering Dad's funny bone, as he kept on laughing. I felt myself go crimson. He did not say anything to break the tension, which made me only try harder. I tried pushing him to the wall again. He only pushed back.

We wrestled around for a bit, Dad laughing the whole time. He was laughing at me and I hated him. He pushed me back harder and dropped his left and threw back his head to laugh and spew his putrid breath at me again. He said, "This must be the bad fish sticks."

I was done. With his hand down, I threw the punch I had always dreamed of throwing. It started around my shoelaces and made a wide loop toward his chin. I wanted respect from him.

I think every son goes through this at one point or another. It is a place where the child becomes a man by overcoming obstacles and stacking a claim of respect after maneuvering past the trials and tribulations and fifty other clichés. All of those dishonors all rolled into the same tightly clenched fist tensioned through my chest and shoulder and sprung toward his face. I felt the burning in my eyes and the fear of what would happen after I connected with his jaw, but I did not care. I had been practicing a punch like this since Dad took me out into the backyard when I was seven. Now the same knowledge he used to educate me turned against him. He was off balance, crude, and drunk. He needed to get cracked. Things happened in slow motion when I threw that punch at my father. I would think of it as a marked occasion in my development as a person, a time to celebrate.

Dad's reaction, however, was not as I had hoped. His dropped left hand came back up. His stumbling posture righted itself and my fist hit his well-calloused hand and stopped it. With his other hand, he snapped off a punch that traveled three inches and hit me dead center in the chest with a hollow thump. The oxygen left my body all at once as I crumpled and somersaulted backward, landing under the dining room table.

I heard Dad laugh in the darkness.

He once told me, "I remember a bigger guy beat your father up once. I followed him home with a pipe and cracked him with it when his back was turned. Not to kill 'im, just to make him see stars. No Marquess of Queensbury. No fair fight. When he was on the ground, I stood over him, because I wanted him to know who did it. I wanted him to know that I was not fucking around."

I wanted a pipe. I wanted Dad to turn around just for a minute. Next to the dining room table, Dad still laughed from deep inside. I peeked from under the table. He looked at me and pointed to himself and said, "Man." And then pointed at me and said, "Boy."

***

BEFORE I LEFT THE stadium, I walked back by the archways that led to the seats and saw a ring of orange dirt, which looked delicious, like pound cake, and reminded me of baseball.

Dad and I had gone to see the Dodgers when I was a kid. On special occasions, he would scrounge up tickets the day of the game and give me five minutes to get ready after he announced we had seats on the first-base side. I would grab my wrong-handed glove and we would jump in his van and race out the door.

Sure, Dad and I had the Olympic as an underground world and an extension of Alvarado and Eighth Street when I was younger. I loved it because I thought it connected to Dad's world. As I got a little older, baseball took over.

Baseball was different. It was clean, bright, intelligent, and professional. The Olympic and its events were dark, seedy, hidden, and off the grid. I aspired to the former; it was the latter that made me feel more alive. Bullfighting, I would decide, was a complex mixture of both worlds.

In this way, bullfighting was less like the aggression of boxing and roller derby and more cerebral, like baseball. Eventually, the bull goes down for the long count to be sliced into lean fillets by dawn, but it was the *how* and *technique* that brought smartness to death.

However, what I remembered most about the bullfights was walking through the arena's long tunnel and out into the stadium. In baseball, there was something magical about walking out and seeing the field. The outfield grass was freshly cut into checkerboard patterns of two shades of surrealist green. Sparkling white bases contrasted against orange dirt base paths. The sky was black from the millions of lights that blotted out the stars, which lit the enthusiastic crowd, whose cheers echoed through me. I never stopped finding that first sight of walking out of the tunnel and seeing the ball field emerge in pieces through the heads of crowd that towered over me magical—no matter how many baseball games I saw. I would be covered with peanut shells by the third inning and anxious for a foul ball to fall into my lap.

It was only after the bullfights, as I walked back to my hotel, that I felt the amount of work Dad did in attempting to connect to my world. Dad bought piles of books and silly packages with cardboard shots of my heroes and thin, inflexible slabs coated with sugar that represented gum. He pulled them out of his pockets as he bent down to me. And he watched me revel in the delirium of trading cards.

I'd sift through the cards like I squeezed out golden toothpaste from an enchanted tube. Carefully, revealing only a tiny bit of the baseball card at a time, I built the anticipation with each new player by teasing myself. A red edge might appear, giving me a clue to which team the player was on. Dad's weight and breath shadowed over me as he peered into my little world. As each player revealed himself, I had player stats and history on the tip of my tongue.

"Who did you get?" he'd ask.

I knew every player from endless nights listening to games on the radio in the living room, at a time when radios were furniture with built-in speakers weighing five hundred pounds.

However, it was not only the baseball cards. Dad was the coach of my first year in Little League, when I was twelve, in the spring of 1979. I could catch but was usually the smallest kid on the field and could not hit my weight, which was miniscule. That year with Dad as coach, I hit .000. I fouled a few off into the chain-link fence behind home plate. I walked a few times, and once I even leaned into a fastball, inspired by the pregame Valium I had taken. Every time, I kicked the dirt and walked away from the plate. Every time, he met me in front of the dugout and put his arm around me. With Dad, there was always a next time, but coaching and baseball were never his thing, unless it was to talk about Ernie Banks.

"Hey, you, fat kid. Yes, you. Looney Tunes. What the hell is this kid's name," he said to the ether. "Play third base," Dad called from the dugout drinking a beer. Dad never understood why he didn't connect with the other kids, and my batting average went up .400 points the year he left.

Chapter 4

I WALKED OUT OF the train station and pulled my rolling suitcase and my father behind me, in a hurry to find my first appointment in Cádiz—Cádiz Tourism—even though it scared me. It was where I needed to reveal my secret about bringing Dad and finishing his quest. I needed a perfect place to scatter him. I needed a singer for "Ave Maria." I needed to write him a eulogy. I needed to put my entire relationship with him in some sort of unemotional perspective—I assume for mythical closure, where endings came with a fancy bow. The air was crisp, but I began to sweat.

My suitcase rattled across Cádiz's cobblestone sidewalk. I had a map and an address. The beautiful people, who appeared everywhere I looked in Sevilla, were in hiding, as the regular shop owners took to the foreground with their windswept hair and imperfect expressions.

I did my best to mimic the overly casual energy of the locals. Every block or two of aimless walking, I stopped to attempt map reading and orient myself. I heard gulls and lapping waves, which I imagined called a welcome to Dad. The wind consistently folded the map upon itself as I tried to find where I stood. Then I walked some more along roads that twisted and turned without reason.

I like logical city grids with bold addresses that make getting lost impossible, the need to ask for directions unnecessary. Southern Spain, as well as much of Europe, is the antithesis. Roads curve and meander and rarely represent anything symmetrical. Street addresses are microscopic and might not be in numerical order. City blocks appear to have been giant lumps of clay that fell from the sky and landed in a splat, forming misshapen areas where people came and built houses a thousand years ago. Cádiz was proving an adventure, and I had not even started yet.

After half an hour, I discovered I had walked in a circle. The experience was somehow wonderful. I was lost and forced myself to stop every person in my path to show them my address and map. I used body language and said, *"Pardon, mi espanol es muy malo"* often. They wore light sweaters and aprons, name badges, and a willingness to chat with me. No one had exact directions, but they all knew I was on the right track. Everyone had a smile and the time to help a stranger. An older woman with gray hair, wrapped in a red shawl, who spoke no English, simply handed me a baguette, patted me on the forearm, and kept walking.

I later found out that the city of Cádiz is broken up into two parts: the "New" part, featuring tall, five-star digs and not enough parking, and the "Old" part, which features traditional courtly charm, afternoon siestas—and not enough parking. I was excited not only to be in a new city, but because this was it. I brought Dad back to his mysterious/phony past.

After twenty more minutes, I stumbled into an unassuming building near the water. The elevator opened into the fourth floor and directly into the office of Cádiz Tourism. The sound of keyboards clattering was overshadowed only by the enthusiastic Spanish voices that said whatever it is that they said in the office of eight people. I stood for a moment and felt a warm flash across my face and waited for someone to help me. I finally cleared my throat at the closest desk to the elevator. *"Hola, me llamo es Devin de Los Angeles."*

The pretty receptionist smiled and said, *"Un momento,"* and walked away.

I was about to confess the real nature of my trip, and a knot tightened in my stomach. The secretary returned a minute or two later with her boss—a short, gruff-looking woman in her early forties. She first shook my hand and then kissed me on either cheek and introduced herself as Juanita, a woman's name I heard many times in previous days in Spain and would hear more of in the coming ones.

Juanita clapped her hands together, saying something in Spanish to the room. All the clattering of keyboards and office chatter stopped. Writing travel articles is a little like being a minor celebrity, and I was used to this sort of pending introduction. Tourism folks know that their job is to make my life simple and fantastic so that I will, in turn, write glowing things about their city, hotels, attractions, whatever. The ladies approached first with alternating cheek kisses, before the men offered handshakes weaker than Americans thought normal.

After all the formal introductions, Juanita presented my itinerary in a manila envelope. I was to be given a car and then I would spend the better part of the upcoming week cruising through Andalucia. There would be hilltop villages slathered in whitewash that appeared to be right off a postcard, vine-ripened bodegas, family-owned B&Bs, and each, I imagined, with a black-vested Geppetto-like character taking care of the grounds. It all sounded great. As Juanita hunched over my itinerary and several office staff formed a small semicircle around us, I wondered, maybe *this* was Dad's last joyride? I felt a little bit of happiness, like I was doing something good for him. Maybe he was looking down at us and grateful for the opportunity. I placed my itinerary back into the manila envelope and tucked it under my arm.

The formality of business faded. I heard a couple of relaxed sighs and saw a couple of postures soften. A few Cádiz staff stayed to ask me questions about myself and my family.

"Where do you live?" Anna asked. She wore a pantsuit and had long, dark hair held in a ponytail.

Daria said, "I have been to Los Angeles once," and then asked, "Is this your first time in Spain? What do you think of it?" Daria had shoulder-length, curly light brown hair and an earthy, unpretentious glow that made me suck in my stomach and push out my chest.

The questions and conversation continued and flowed in a relaxed way from my new Spanish friends, as I felt progressively more anxiety. I abruptly pointed at my bag—after all, the secret portion of my mission was over, and I needed help. I raised my arm and swung it around to point at my rolling suitcase a few feet away and told them all, *"Mi padre is muerto in la bolsa."* I continued, *"Necessito cantante para 'Ave Maria' tambien."* I had no idea whether or not what I had said made much sense to them. I hoped they would piece everything together so I did not have to repeat myself. My face went scarlet. I held my arm out like I was a model on *The Price is Right*. I held my breath and waited.

I watched as they looked at each other, then to me, and then at my suitcase for about thirty seconds of collective bewilderment. Juanita asked, "What do you mean your father is dead in the bag? And you need a singer for 'Ave Maria'?"

As she spoke, I took a deep breath and felt less red. I bent down and began to unzip my suitcase, when Juanita waved her hands frantically to stop me from what I was doing while the rest of her crew began to lean in for a closer look. I relished in the absurdity of the moment, and my anxiety disappeared.

There were dramatic expressions and wide eyes. I began to tell them the whole story, even the unsolved mystery of my father's desire to be set adrift in Spain. The group reaction—slacked jaws and wide smiles—garnered me extra double-kisses from the ladies and a hug from Daria, my new point of contact while I traveled. Cesar, the web designer, also came up to me, putting his arm around me, and said, "Don't worry, we will help you through this," which felt ironic. I mean, what was there to help? I was in Spain and carrying around my dead father while sorting out a lifetime of questionable history.

I was handed the keys of a tiny blue car and given instructions to my first destination, about two hours away. I called to the room as I was leaving, "Please find me a singer, so I can scatter my dad." As I turned toward the elevator, my brain clicked into overdrive, desperate to connect all the puzzle pieces. I left with the glow of new friends and their assurances that they would find a singer, but I was certain that their kindness meant little to them. They probably offered similar support to every writer who blew through town.

***

HE CAUGHT MY PUNCH the same way my mitt stopped soft tennis balls that sprung from the front porch steps when I practiced grounders. It was a low point between Dad and me. The worst part about the event was that it meant nothing to him. He woke up the next morning and went about his day. He never commented on it again.

I, on the other hand, sulked in my closet for a week. In the closet, I had my records, an old record player, a drawer half-full of airplane miniatures of rum, and a pillow shaped like the back of a chair that let me lean against the wall and have deep thoughts that filled up the closet.

I forgave him the first time I needed an extra twenty.

I graduated high school weighing 122 pounds and standing at five feet nine. My skin remained an adolescent mess of acne and irritated redness, which I treated with every kind of Stridex pad, antibacterial roll-on, medicinal cleanser, and ointment, in addition to washing compulsively. Most days I was uncomfortable. My face burned, and I was as awkward as I looked. I remember taking a class from a rabbi who suggested that acne is caused by telling lies. On bad days, I slathered my face with a heavy coat of Noxema, which accomplished nothing beyond hiding my face behind a layer of tingly sour cream. I took painkillers and refused to leave my room, and it never occurred to me to tell the truth.

I should have been thinking about college. College felt more like an idea rather than a plan, like a birthday. I expected a letter with a fancy embossed logo to show up at my door that read: "We have heard good things about you and can see beyond your 2.0 grade point average. Welcome to college. Don't worry, we have taken care of everything. Show up at your leisure in September. We have taken the liberty to sign you up for all your favorite classes. We have also picked out a nice girl from the Midwest with frosted hair and acid-wash jeans. She will not think you are lame for spending most of your time eating muscle relaxants and listening to Billy Joel records. Sincerely, Harvard, Yale, and Princeton (take your pick)."

The admissions letter never showed up. Instead, I enrolled at a local junior college when the lone university I applied to never panned out. However, all wasn't lost.

I rewarded my graduation, on my eighteenth birthday, by moving into my room a wooden, square ashtray with a shiny metal trapdoor top that dropped cigarette butts and ash into a hidden compartment—

it was all so 1960s retro, and I was growing wings. I bought cheap leather loafers with tassels to contrast Dad's work boots and walked around like I owned a yacht. I swaggered into my parents' bedroom to tell my dad the news of my open-smoking liberation.

After all, Mom accepted the news, five minutes prior, quite well. She was in the kitchen eating soup over the oven, right from the pot. I don't think she even turned to face me. "Ugh," she said. "Well, how surprised could I be?"

I waited a moment for any secondary reaction, taking a swallow of milk from the carton as I paused by the refrigerator. I heard the sounds of soup slurping. "Okay, so I am just going to start smoking in my room," I said, and left to let Dad know the good news. I assumed he would love the idea.

"You, the fuck, what?!" He had been lying shirtless, watching a rerun of *Bonanza* or some other show with technicolor cowboys. He turned to sit up, and I knew to run. I could feel it. I sprinted down the hall and out the front door, hearing his feet pound on the floor after me. I ran down the block, glad that he was fat and glad I was not on weed and downers.

When I got about five houses down, I turned and saw him in front of the house, hands on his hips, bent over, sucking wind. The subject of me smoking cigarettes was never debated again. In the evening, I enjoyed my first legal cigarettes in my life in the coziness of my own space.

As much as Dad hated the idea of me smoking, he began to accept me as a grown-up capable of making just as many stupid decisions as he did. This led to the sharing of the most magical of uniting forces: alcohol.

On the way home from an afternoon of sweeping out an empty apartment, Dad pulled into the parking lot of Tom Bergin's House of Irish Coffee. The name rang a bell. It was a local cop bar that Dad had referred to once in a while. By that time, I had also admitted to drinking. Dad opened the van door and stepped out. I did not move a muscle, thinking this was a trap. While he had accepted my grown-up decisions, I was far from trusting. "Well," he said. "What are you waiting for?"

I sat looking at Dad, trying to size up the situation. "Dad, I am underage. Should I wait in the car?"

"What are you, weird?" he said. "Come on."

Bergin's walls were covered in hand-painted green clovers with the white letters of the names of the many patrons who had become regulars over the years. The clovers nearly covered every inch of available wall and ceiling space from Bergin's seventy years of business. Bright green-and-white clovers became smoke-stained brown-and-olive-toned within a year. The rectangular bar was dark, with tall wooden benches bolted to the ground, and uncomfortable until about the sixth pint of lager. The background chatter filled the room and always felt lighthearted. I loved Bergin's, mostly because it was Dad's bar. Walking through the front door with him for the first time was surreal, in much the same way as when Dorothy walked out of her relocated, brown Kansas home into a vibrant Munchkinland.

The bartender wore a white dress shirt and a green tie. He was sixty, gray, and had a stomach that required pants with an expandable waist. He had powder-blue eyes and plump, rosy, spider-veined cheeks. As Dad and I walked in, he eyed us with suspicion.

"You again," he said with an Irish accent and sneered toward Dad, who sheepishly pointed to himself and then slowly looked around him acting like "Who, me?" The bartender continued, "I have already told you never to come back, never to darken this fine establishment's doorway. How dare you? Should I get the bat?" He reached under the bar while maintaining eye contact with Dad. I held my breath, ready to run toward the exit. I felt the warm sensation of panic rise up from my stomach and fill my face, flushed with underage guilt. Dad stared at the bartender and the bartender stared back at Dad. I looked back and forth to them both. A moment later, Dad put both his hands on his belly and laughed hard. Dad said, "This is Michael, the worst fucking tender in all of Los Angeles." Dad then reached across the bar and hugged Michael across the shoulders.

Michael smiled wide and turned toward me. "You must be the kid," he said, sticking out his hand. Michael had a strong, powerful grip. "I have heard a lot about you."

Dad said, "He'll have a Budweiser."

Michael said, "Do you let your father order for you all the time?"

I smiled and cleared my throat and croaked out, "Just this once."

It was on the barstools of Bergin's that I began to see Dad as a man rather than the hero or villain. He became something beyond a mere jerk. I watched how he interacted with those around him. He lit everyone's cigarette, hugged everyone he met. He had an endless stream of acquaintances and not a single bad thing to say about anyone. As he loosened up, he began to talk about women differently, with a chiding elbow into my ribs, "Did you catch the cans on that fucking broad?" The fact that he spoke about women outside of his marriage to my mother made no dent in my ethical understanding. I was part of the cool guys, sitting in a bar talking about "broads."

Over time, I began to unravel his moral code from my seat at the bar. I began to understand that he had no moral code. He never directly admitted to anything, but he enjoyed people, even if he didn't seem to trust them. It was all about word choice. To some degree, his life was just as murky to me as ever. He never knew anyone well. He just "met" a guy. He never bought or stole things. He "found" them. I remember one morning waking up to him sitting on the coffee table. There were twenty-five pieces of pristine Roseville pottery, popular, collectible, hard to find, and expensive.

I knew about the Roseville because Dad had opened a small furniture shop called Nothing's New, a name my mother made up and still takes credit for its double-entrendre'd genius. The store was small, with one large window in the front. Inside the walls were lines with old steamer trunks, dressers, desks, tables, nightstands, vanities, and chairs. When the store was full, furniture was stacked three layers high with a middle aisle. On top of every flat surface were small sets of colored Depression glass and bud vases and old glasses or postcards, and anything else that could make a little money. The store opened at a time when antiques were particularly hip. Dad scoured antiques books to learn and develop an eye for the good stuff, although I am not sure he cared. He liked the "thrill of the hunt."

He talked about the newly discovered treasures almost compulsively. It was also one of the few things we did as a family.

We had been junking for years. Dad knew most of the dealers from all the times he sold our furniture or had to restock the living room. They all had gaunt faces with bags under their eyes. I discovered their worn-out expressions came from the hunt for the career-ending find of a priceless heirloom that would fetch millions at auction. The prospect never overcame the reality. Junking was a full-time job that saw Dad and me sifting through boxes with a flashlight in the dark and in the back of someone's pickup truck before the swap meet started.

Of course, most of Dad's finds came from other sources unknown.

Dad's eyes were jaundiced and glassy, and he smelled of Budweiser. He tapped out a Salem regular before pulling out another to light. Before I said anything, Dad said, "Look what I found," and waved his arm across the sea of pottery, plastic bags, and crumpled newspaper balls that sat on the floor of the living room. I took a moment to absorb the scene. Dad had found many things in quantity in the past: multiple sets of skis, African masks, paintings, brass beds, even some oil wells along La Cienega Boulevard. This became the first time I questioned his finds, just shortly before I started working for him. "Dad," I said with a hint of sarcasm, "you just found twenty-five pristine pieces of Roseville pottery? That seems impossible. Did you rob someone?"

I did not expect an answer.

Dad looked at me and the amber tip of his cigarette glowed orange as he dragged in nicotine. "I have some more in the trunk. I know this guy. And what the fuck is it to you?" Then he smiled wide as if he let me in on part of a secret. Truth is, he seldom let me in on the secret, but his smirks let me know there was more to the story, which was more than most got. His smirk meant that the Roseville would be sold at far less than its value at Nothing's New.

He started the store with a former neighbor and local muscle named Manny, who collected owed money under the cloak of darkness for businesses in the area. Manny had teeth the color of phlegm. He had dark skin and light eyes. His crooked nose trailed off to the left side of his face. He had big round shoulders, an Afro—though I was pretty sure he was white—and a gut that rivaled Dad's. Manny was forever pulling up his pants from falling down. He also enjoyed

cocaine. In many ways, he was like Dad. Manny became indebted to
Dad after Dad bailed Manny out of jail for pimping and pandering.

Oddly, I loved Manny.

Even when I was young, I knew he was impulsive and unstable.
Dad was a thug out of necessity from a lack of education and
schooling, but Manny would have been a criminal under the most
fortunate of circumstances. It was his calling. Still, there had always
been a sense that Manny and Dad had an honorable agreement both
based upon years of knowing each other and often dissolved at a
moment's notice. They made up just as quickly. Manny was also our
next-door neighbor.

Of course, Dad and Manny's business relationship soured quickly
and required police intervention. Dad kept the store and Manny kept
a few bucks as something that resembled a buyout. Without many
prospects, I was ushered into the fold.

Nothing's New taught me about life and my first real lesson
came when I found Dad with an African-looking statue in the large
parking area behind the store. We had just bought ten pieces of art
and several strands of colorful beads from a tall African man who
claimed to be a prince from Nigeria.

The statue was a primitive wood carving of a nude male with a
huge dangling schlong. It had been painted black, except where the
one of its long feet had been broken off.

Pointing at the break, "Do we have the foot so we can glue it
back on?" I said.

He looked at me with a half smirk, "What are you, weird?"
He reached down and grabbed a small handful of brown dirt from a
dry puddle and rubbed it on the break to darken it. Then he snapped
off the other foot and applied more dirt to the whole statue. He pulled
over the hose and splatted the statue with water and then rubbed in
more dirt. He motioned me inside the store and then closed the back
door behind him, leaving the statue in the sun.

Within a couple of days, a man came into the store and picked up
the statue. He tried to stand it up while he called to the back, where
Dad polished a glass and I sat drinking a beer. "What happened to
the statue?"

Dad walked to the front of the store, still cleaning the glass. "It's from the Bumbura Tribe from Mali," Dad said and smiled. "It's an interesting story. This is a ceremonial burial idol. When someone died in the village, they would carve a doll like this and bury it with the body..."

The man interrupted, "Yes, but what about the feet? It's broken."

"No," Dad said, "it is done on purpose. It is something the Bumburas did for only the most important people in the tribe." Dad took the statue from the man and turned it around carefully eyeing the figure. "This guy is probably a chief or a medicine man. It is hard to know from these markings." Dad looked up to the man. "They broke off the feet so the soul never wandered away from the village."

Pretty soon, one by one, all our African art had a tale attached after they were dirtied up. I learned the art of the story.

***

I BOUGHT THE BIGGEST sunglasses I could find at the Oklahoma City airport to cover my black eye. I also parted my hair on the side to let my long hair fall across my face. Sort of like when I used to wear a twisted bandana around my neck anytime I received a hicky. My eye had swollen purple and yellow, and the bruising started at the top of my cheek and ended around the upper corners of my left eye. I could open and close it a little, but the dull ache at every blink reminded me that I had been punched in the face to go along with several other purple-and-yellow marks that decorated my body that had been hit. Then I sat in economy class of a Delta Airlines flight back to Los Angeles, the nonstop air-conditioning drying out my sinuses and aggravating my eye.

Dad waited for me in the airport lounge in the bar area just outside the gate. It was during a dreamy time in history when family could still meet their loved ones at the airport, in the terminal, drinking alcohol at a makeshift bar. It was a time of innocence.

As I made my way down the tunnel from the airplane into the terminal, and before my eyes adjusted to the fluorescent lights of LAX, I could hear my father's voice above all the airport chatter.

"I knew they would hate you in Oklahoma," he said. The hair on the back of my neck bristled. "How could they not hate you?" he continued. I still hadn't made it out of the gate but saw him laughing, holding his stomach.

I wished I had a better story for Dad, something that started over something worth fighting over. In my fantasy bar fight scene, there would be a stare down, no blinking allowed. Patrons would whisper among themselves about the new guy looking at Tex, or some other name for a regional tough guy. The drunks at the bar would surround us like a schoolyard circle and we would then circle around each other, feeling each other out before any punch was thrown. Master Ito, a three-hundred-year-old Japanese martial arts master, who was my sensei, would accompany me. His ability to communicate with me telepathically would help me in my dismantling of all my enemies.

I had always wanted a bar fight on my résumé, something that would initiate me into a ready-for-anything manhood club. Nothing like that ever took place.

I stood at the Round Up, a cowboy bar with sawdust and peanuts shells on the floor, and tried to ignore the generic country band playing Willie Nelson covers while I prayed some girl would start a conversation with me. There was smoke in the air, colored lights, and lots of people. It was the perfect climate for a headache.

I nursed my beer belly up to the bar when a cowboy came up to the waitress station where I stood and hit me in the face, hard. Not knockout-power hard, but surprising and jarring; I didn't see it coming. The kind of hard that snapped reality into a fuzzy dream state where an assessing voice took over.

I have just been punched in the face? No, I am not dead, but my left eye throbs. Do I know this person who just punched me? Why did he punch me? I was just standing here listening to this crappy country band. He is still standing here. He just punched me in the face again. This is all very confusing and upsetting. I should do something before he punches me in the face some more. I don't like being punched in the face.

The conversation lasted a split second before I took action toward the cowboy hat and plaid shirt.

At the airport bar, Dad didn't move. He sat there, slowly swirling the beer suds around in a tall glass as I slowly walked up. He had a huge sly grin. "You make your father laugh," he said, and he let out a huge laugh and took a drag off a Salem regular. I hated his laugh. It was always at someone else's expense. I hoped he choked on the cigarette. So I lit a cigarette to punish him by smoking at him—it was my way of saying "fuck you." I had not had a cigarette since I left Oklahoma City. I was nuts without nicotine.

He said, "Okay, I knew you would have to be smart with one of those fucking hay-bailing types from some farm who was not interested in your mouth. Did you at least get in a punch? Something? Anything? Tell me something good. Did you represent your father well?"

I sheepishly looked at the ground. Dad then laughed wildly. "Well, no. I tried to hit him with a barstool," I said. Dad narrowed his eyes at me like he was looking at something tiny. "The fucking guy just cracked me. I was just standing there having a beer, and bam."

It was only after I was on the plane that I realized that the Round Up of Oklahoma City probably had ample history that required the barstools to be screwed into the ground.

"I guess we punched each other a little and then started wrestling," I told Dad. "Then a whole bunch of guys wearing matching T-shirts pulled us apart and dragged me outside."

I looked at the floor and avoided Dad's amusement.

I was angry I got knocked around and proud-ish of the experience. I told Dad, "They said *my kind* was not appreciated in their establishment. What kind of shit is that? Then they stood there watching me and I walked back to that dump I stayed in a couple of blocks away." I was stunned, angry, and bloodied from a cut inside my lip. I felt tougher, and proud that I didn't get a bigger whooping from a cowboy wearing a real cowboy hat and a bolo tie, a tie I dreamed of strangling him with later that night.

I gazed into the mirror in my motel bathroom. The blood in my face pulsed as a badge of honor, and I watched my eye swell closed. I experienced the rush of my first barroom brawl. It was not much, but it was mine.

I took up boxing and some martial arts in the years that followed, under the illusion that I liked it. This changed after many "whomp" sounds that clanged against my head during every sparring session. I sucked at fighting.

However, when I stood in front of Dad in the airport lounge, I just felt like a knucklehead who had been punched out by a cowboy in Oklahoma, without a redeeming story.

"Yeah, Dad, you should see the other guy." To this and my pathetic delivery, Dad laughed even louder, and reached across the table, wafting cigarette smoke across my nose, and gave my shoulder a squeeze before pulling my large sunglasses away from my face.

"You fool, you don't fight with a bar stool in a bar, you fucking jerk. Stick a lit cigarette in the guy's eye." With his reassuring arm around me, we walked toward the exit. "Did you at least get some broad to blow you?"

"Sure, Dad," I told him, even though we both knew it was bullshit.

Dad was right about the fighting part of it. He always told me to avoid wasting energy, get scary before the other guy does. Stick a cigarette in his eye. Break a glass in his face and move on. He had told me stuff like that twenty times. If the fight would have taken place at home in town, I know what his advice would have been. Wait a week and hit him with a hammer on the back of his head. Just fuck him up. When he was on the ground, make sure he knew who had hit him, then hit him some more.

My eyes burned as I stood in the middle of the airport feeling bruised and confronted by my thug father, who would have handled himself so much better and broken a bottle into a guy's face before moving on. The proud-ish-ness waned. Why did I feel like a moron? Still, I wore the Eskimo Joe's commemorative tank top until it was rotting off my back fifteen years later.

As we walked toward baggage claim at LAX, he dangled his set of store keys from Nothing's New in front of my face. "Oh, by the way, Mr. Kickass," he laughed. "Here are my keys to the store. I won't be needing them. I am giving you the store and I am leaving your mother"—a statement my mother would contest, demanding that it was *she* who actually threw *him* out. His words rattled in my ears and I tried to make sense out of what he had just said.

While I grew up in a house with the dreadful constant of jagged arguing or unyielding quiet, I never considered that my parents would actually break up. Their otherworldly bond seemed based on rules outside the system of human logic. I could never see either of them with anyone else.

Their separation made sense and was long overdue. Unfortunately, I didn't want to work. Selling stories was fun, but who had time for a store? My own life had been consumed by higher priorities: chain-smoking, vodka, stolen pills, ten-dollar games of seven-card stud, fast food, and the never-ending quest for an angelic slut.

I ran around with a fake ID I purchased at the Clovis Flea Market outside of Fresno, California. I used the name Drake Valentine.

Drake was the divinely inspired name that intended to be the older, smoother, and more confident version of myself. The ID was two for five dollars, and had a hand-drawn, patriotic-looking eagle in the center and a birth date ten years older than mine, with my baby-faced smirk in the upper left. For credibility, my new identification was laminated. Drake would not be caught dead at the Clovis Flea Market, but the ID worked all over the Pacific Northwest, until a bouncer from a bar catering to obese white women who wanted to hook up with black guys checked my ID against a book picturing all known California identification cards. "Sorry, man. I can't give this back to you." The second card was thrown out of a car when I thought a cop was going to pull me over and I got paranoid. Drake would now be in his late fifties, but likely dead from venereal disease if I could match the intention of his inspiration.

I eventually smashed the golden end of a lit smoke out in someone's face. It was after getting a trim at Supercuts during an overcast day. The hot embers flashed across my knuckles and burned the back of my hand. I saw the black smudge across his cheek as we were pulled apart by others getting a haircut. It was pointless. I ran home before the police could arrive. Like most things from Dad's world, it was an acquired taste with little payoff.

I just kept thinking I was doing life wrong, but I was willing to learn anything to be a man, like Dad.

***

IT WAS A LONE hour in Vegas doing what I loved that changed our relationship for the worse, forever—when we sat at a poker table for the first time together.

From the time I was sixteen, I dealt out hands of seven-card stud, face up, on the floor of my room. One hand to me and four-to-six hands to invisible, hypothetical players. Between the silence, the tactile feel of the slippery plastic cards shuffled, fanned, and dealt, and the meditation on a single question: What would I need to do to win—regardless of the real strength of the cards I had? The allure was intellectual satisfaction and romantic—almost as good as sneaking cigarettes and eating sedatives. There was also a more practical reason: I wanted to have gambling stories.

Dad's shadowy gambling exploits may have been my first drug. When I was little, he would return from Vegas with a small green-and-pink souvenir slot machine and maybe a pair of red-and-white Vegas dice. His stories came from his dealings in big casinos and smoky card rooms, or with bookies and bruisers, amateurs and pros.

While his stories had a vagueness of details, I filled in the cracks with my imagination. The situations sounded dangerous, exhilarating, but a place for men to earn respect by just being there and a possible way to get Dad's respect. Only a badass walked Dad's path. I was a twig but had a rich fantasy life. From the first time I could convince him to tell me about a casino, I knew that was what and where I wanted to be—a man earning his stripes as a gambler.

So I dealt out hands on the floor and looked for ways to understand the odds and probabilities. I read books about body language and the individual strategies for every version of poker. By the time I was twenty, I had played in most of the local card rooms in town and a few in Vegas. I learned quickly, and though I was never a great player, I knew how to get up and leave with more chips than I'd started with. Within a couple of years, I had fared well

My father (bottom left) and his siblings, three sets of twins, in 1936.

My father (top right) and his siblings approximately twelve years after the above.

My young and snazzy father.

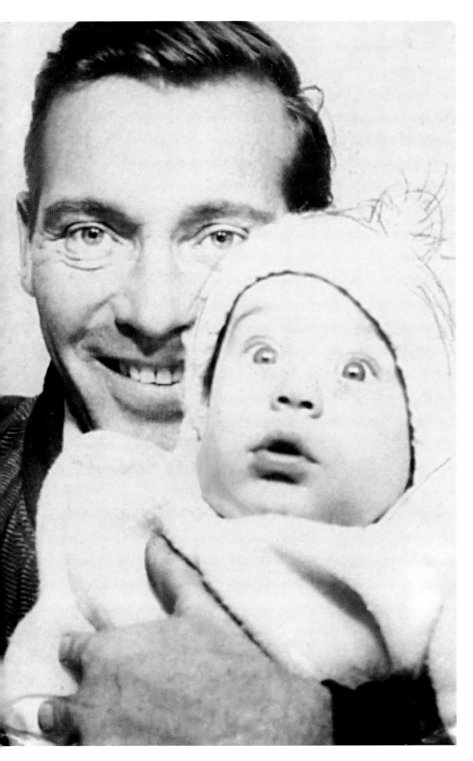

Dad and Baby Devin in 1966.

Dad and me outside the house I grew up in, 1970.
My absolute favorite picture of us together.

Fun in the desert with Dad in 1970.

*Me with my irrepressible grandma, Dad, and his twin
in front of the house I grew up in.*

*Fresh faced with Grandma, Dad, and my aunt
on a cross-country trip to Arlington Heights, Illinois, 1981.*

*The last photo of me, Mom, and Dad together
at my high school graduation, Los Angeles, California, 1984.*

Along the coast in Old Town Cádiz, Spain, with new friends, 2005.

in small tournaments and played solid in ring games in casinos and home games. I even began to count cards in blackjack.

With Dad living in Las Vegas and me confident in my card-playing ability, I wanted to show off and garner mock esteem from Dad, to show I had somehow arrived as an adult.

"I have a proposition," I told him. "I know this seven-card game over at Bally's. Why don't we buy in for a tray each, blow up the game, and move on to the Mirage"—the best card room on the strip, at the time—"for a little fun with someone else's money at a larger game?"

Bally's was a dud of a casino, but it had a regular $5/$10 stud game and attracted players who wanted to splurge on their poker experience, who did well playing cards in their aunt's living room.

"What are you, weird?" Dad said. I assumed he thought that he would take my money and would feel guilty if he stole his son's bankroll. To me it was worth the risk. I convinced him I could handle the loss.

We walked into the endless sounds of the plinks and blongs and coins falling on each other from an island of slot machines at a time before casino technology went coin-free. The casino was not crowded and made the busy, multicolored casino carpet, dim-glitz lighting, and neon dizzying. Regardless of how they are marketed, the best casinos are lonely places that need to seem glamorous to those who are alone, as a justification. When we arrived at the poker room, a roped-off section of the casino floor surrounded by more slot machines, there were several games going, mostly low-stakes hold 'em.

Around the tables were a collection of fat locals who ate meals at the table and rarely played a hand unless they had a pair of aces to raise with, and a few scattered tourists who just wanted to feel what it was like to play poker with real poker players. These folks played too many hands and ultimately were frightened by seeing lots of chips pushed into the center of the table. Dad and I waited about thirty minutes for a couple of empty seats at the ten-dollar table.

We sat at opposite ends of the green oval felt table, with me on one far end while he sat close to the dealer. My strategy was simple. Watch the game for about half an hour, see who knew how to play and who didn't. I planned to make many loud comments about the poor play of everyone at the table and flash my bad collection of rings on every finger: the lumpy gold nugget ring, the ring of intertwining horseshoes with ruby-colored rhinestones, the class ring of some frat boy that I stole at a bar when he took it off from some drinking game. I wore dark sunglasses. Everything I did was done by design to be a nuisance or a distraction. It was subtle and effective. "Is this the game where one pair beats two pairs? Because they do that at some casinos," I asked the table as the first hand was dealt.

Dad played the first hand against two others. Dad was showing a six. I watched closely. Trying to learn from his experience and skill. By the end of the hand, Dad had called bets in every round before weakly throwing away his hand. He shrugged his shoulders at me and said, "Missed." It didn't look like he had a straight or flush draw.

Obviously, it was all for show. He wanted to look weak. It might have cost him a hundred to call a few bets, but it would likely come back when he started to play strong. I thought, *Wow! He must be a great card player, because he sure looks like an idiot.* I scooted my chair closer to the table for a better look.

The next three hands all played out the same as the first. Dad called multiple bets before folding at the end. He ordered a Budweiser, lit up a cigarette, looked confident, and pulled out several more hundred dollars to fill the empty space in front of him where chips were supposed to be. I ached in the pit of my stomach. I wanted to believe that this was all part of a larger ruse, but I could tell it wasn't. That's when I realized all of his drinking and mindless splashing of chips into the pot with absolutely no chance of winning was not an act. My heart began to pound like I was on a sinking ship. Over the next hour, Dad tanked and quickly blew through a grand of crumpled hundreds. Dad sat there laughing, smiling, clinking glasses with another loser next to him. My throat burned as I suppressed tears. I slumped in my chair, so caught up in Dad's failure that whatever competitive spark I had was quickly doused.

He went from smart hustler, the way I had seen him my whole life, to obsessed action junkie in sixty minutes. I now saw him perhaps for the first time. He was not merely an idiot in a tongue-in-cheek way, in a way I could laugh with him about being a lovable rogue. But I saw him as something far worse than a liar and a cheat. He was a mark. Every illusion I had of him shattered into a million pieces. I sat there with all my chips in front of me. I did not play a single hand but felt like I had lost everything.

I watched him laugh and drink and puff and call another raise. He was having fun. I folded the next hand without even looking at my cards and walked around the table as Dad flung a few chips into the abyss while he said, "I'm in." I crouched down next to him and took a long drag of smoke. I looked at the floor and waited to be noticed. My hands were clammy and throat dry. He was quietly annoyed by my presence but still played on, until he lost the hand and probably another hundred. When he turned to me, he said, "What do you fucking want from me?"

"Dad, let's not do this. I am not sure I can watch this." There, I said it. The words made me ill. I didn't want to say more than that. Those two sentences should have said everything to him: my sadness, disillusionment, dark view for my future.

He looked confused. "I thought you wanted me to play cards with you?"

I said, "Let me buy you a few drinks."

We both cashed out and then we sat in the hotel bar and had green midori and creams that went down like Lysol with beer chasers.

In the end, I proved nothing to him or myself. If I could do it over, I would stay there and win my portion of his losses.

✳✳✳

Dad ended up not being much of a gambler, but he still had game.

"I wouldn't go over there if I were you," Rick said over the chiming and rattling noises that came from bar-top video poker machines. Rick stared into the bottom of his glass, a small shooter of a beer that could only be served off the Strip in a crappy, wood-paneled bar on a weekday night in Vegas. The place smelled of rust and vomit, where regulars slumped over the bar with confidence that the red-sparkle, vinyl-covered barstools remained empty on either side of them. The walls had red-and-blue flickering neon beer signs and posters of pro sports teams that had seen better days. The chatter of the few talking patrons, whirring ceiling fans, and air-conditioning hum filled the room. I massaged my temples and stared at Dad from across the bar. It was late. Dad and Las Vegas pissed me off.

It had been an hour since Dad excused himself to use the "crapper" and instead plopped himself next to the lone single, attractive female in the building about a minute before I planned to do the same. He wore an untucked dress shirt, brown dress shoes without socks, and a pair of stained green sweatpants. Dad looked homeless.

The young woman Dad sat with was about twenty-four years old and thirty years his junior. She was a cute brunette. Well, cute enough and revealing a bit of cleavage. She looked clean and normal, out of place in that dump, but Dad helped her fit in. He had been putting on a show for her, making funny faces, animated hand gestures. He lit her cigarettes and bought her a tall, fruity drink, then two beers for himself. She was listening, laughing, and occasionally putting her hand on his arm. Dad needed little encouragement. He got her to clink glasses and bottoms up while I watched intently.

I tried to read his lips as I sat across the bar with my uncle Rick. I came to understand that it didn't matter what he said. We had been in that shithole for hours. Dad had an affinity for dive joints, but it only just occurred to me why he liked them.

Places like that bar were uncrowded and dark. The regulars were alcoholic and kept to themselves. The bartenders made little conversation and kept the drinks flowing. Rick looked at the bottom of his glass for only a moment before it was refilled—as if by magic—by invisible bar elves. So too did tiny Dixie cups of stale Brazil nuts arrive out of nowhere. The place smelled of old beer, cigarettes, and stillness. The only motion consisted of occasional souls that wandered toward the jukebox in the corner, to play "Freebird" by Lynyrd Skynyrd to drown out the slot machine noise. The dusty pool table with a single warped cue that sat on its green felt acted as an illusion of activity. All this meant that Dad had the run of the place, and any woman walking through the doors probably had some problems and was sad and alone. It was a place to come to when you did not want to be yourself. Dad knew they needed cheering up. Dad had game. Between gulps of beer, Rick also watched them intently, perhaps studying Dad's moves. Rick had far less game.

"You know, I owe him plenty, but you know how it is." Rick swirled the foam in his glass as he spoke. Rick was my father's youngest brother—half-brother, really, with a shared mother—and was not yet at a state of wretched drunkenness accompanied by slurred speech, finger jabs into my chest, and his opinion of what he really thought about me. His opinions were never complimentary. Rick was short and wide with a growing bald spot on the back of his big, moon-shaped head. I had no idea why I sat there, beyond some distant notion that my family and I were on vacation together and I loved the guy. I waited for Rick to shift gears into belligerency, which, as history showed, happened in a flash.

Rick was rubbing my back and still friendly when he repeated, "Yeah, better not go over there, your dad's working." Rick knew I was annoyed. Dad was fat, actually thirty pounds more beer-soaked than I had ever seen him, probably in the 250 to 260 range and working a lonely girl I'd decided was completely age-inappropriate. "Besides, you're not really up for going over there," Rick said. I had been on an 8,000-calories-a-day diet for a year and bench-pressed until veins popped out of my forehead. I was fit. I wore socks and regular pants. Somehow I still had no game but found the energy to be indignant.

Rick pulled out a ten-dollar bill and laid it on the bar, "Can I get a roll over here, I am fucking lucky." Rick began to play quarter slots at the bar. To me, playing the machines was something like giving up on life. I knew if I were to put in that first quarter, I would want to kill myself within a couple hours.

The only other women in the place were a few hillbillies who might have been attractive twenty-five years ago, before their alcoholism made their mascara permanently pool below their eyes and made their hair lump in a bleached morass on top of their drunken skulls.

As I scanned the room, increasingly pissed that Dad might end up with the only attractive woman in the bar, Rick soured between sips. "No one really likes you," he said to me. "You're only acceptable because of your father." Rick pumped in another five quarters and slammed his fist down on the button to start the machine.

I drank down to the foam of my beer and wiped it off of my mouth with my sleeve before walking over to introduce myself to the lone female in the room, planning to shoo Dad's old ass away in the process. "Thanks for keeping my seat warm, geezer, now skidattle," I planned to say.

But before I even made it all the way to his side of the bar, Dad said, while raising his voice and turning toward me, "There he is. I want to introduce you to my gay son," pointing at me as I came around the corner of the bar. Dad turned toward the brunette. "He has been having a hard time coming out, but I try to love him like he is normal." Then Dad looked down to his beer. "All he does is lift weights and hang around with *those* guys. I want him to be happy, I really do, but this has been a really hard time." The brunette leaned closer to Dad as he continued, "You know, I had such hopes for him when he was little. I am not sure what I did wrong."

The brunette said, "It's not your fault. I bet you were a great dad."

I thought, *what the fuck*, as I stopped dead and went rosy and turned around to walk back to Rick. I had already lost, but not before Dad raised his glass as if to toast me and said, "Be proud, son." I was more in shock than humiliated. And instead of getting angry, I felt admiration. Dad was so seamless and convincing, I almost thought I was homosexual.

It was a shameful twenty-two steps back to my barstool. My beer had been refilled as Rick slammed his fist against the slot machine button. As I sat down, Rick never even looked up. "Did he say you were a fag and make you feel like a loser?" I nodded to agree, and Rick threw a few more quarters into the machine before he said, "Well, you are. You, fucking, I know you. Fuck." I picked up my undersized lager, moved a few barstools away, ordered a paper bowl of chili from the bartender, and nursed a warm beer.

About an hour and three beers later, Dad came over with the brunette on his arm and said, "I have a ride home," and gave me the keys to his fifty-foot-long, chocolate-brown Lincoln Continental with the velour seats. Then he handed me a black (one hundred dollar) chip from the Imperial Palace. He said, "The hundred is for getting rid of Rick." He leaned into my ear. "Put him in a cab and send him to Mars. You, don't come back." I watched as the two of them giggled their way out of the front door.

Now I was saddled with crusty Uncle Rick in the worst bar in America, eating the worst chili in America. Without a better plan, I dumped Rick at a low-rent strip joint with enough money for three beers but not enough for a cab ride back to Dad's place. Rick said, "Fuck you. You and your old man, fuck the both of you."

I said, "I'll be right back, I have to go to the crapper."

By the afternoon of the following day Rick would remember none of it.

I drove around in that big stupid car and tried not to feel alone. I ended up in the Flamingo Hilton to buy cheap weed in the keno lounge. It was easy. I pantomimed with my thumb and forefinger together like I was taking a drag from a doobie and made eye contact with everyone in the room.

"What you looking for?" He had one bushy eyebrow and a dime-bag of skunkweed with my name on it. I smoked out in the middle stall of an all-white toilet with marble floors that smelled of sanitized lemon. I slept in the Lincoln and in the morning went out for heat-lamped pancakes and a fresh pack of cigarettes at Foxy's Firehouse. My eyes were bloodshot and my throat was raw from too much smoke. My chest ached. Two days later, I drove home to Los Angeles and told everyone that I had a great time and that Dad and Rick were doing great.

Chapter 5

MY ITINERARY WAS HECTIC, changing by the moment. Daria from the office of Cádiz Tourism called daily with updates. I thought about Daria often. Our initial meeting was brief and she was only being polite, but I could not help seeing myself lightly holding her hand, our fingers barely intertwined, walking through a path of golden leaves through some park in Spain. It was easy to daydream along the swaying roads of Andalucia, and perhaps not too surprising.

I had used random women to validate me for years. So I pinned the idea of love on Daria, a woman I did not know. The notion that I was still an angry, jittery twig covered with acne persisted long after my life improved both physically and financially.

Andalucia consisted of various hotel stops and lengthy meetings with vice-president-of-marketing types, who sat with me and gave me tapas galore and touted their destination as being more authentic than the last place I had visited, somehow more Spanish, relaxing, idyllic, or corporate.

Oddly, all the hotels I visited were the quintessential part of Spain the industry hoped to project. Hillside converted monasteries that overlooked fields of wine grapes. Quaint fifteenth-century homes divided into unique guest rooms. In all of them, I sat and sipped tea in a courtyard surrounded by overgrown plants. I should have fawned over the delightful quiet and ambiance, but I didn't. The childhood I was given had me feeling sorry for myself about Dad.

I wanted the type of father who would lean with me over the motor of a stalled car and teach me how to fix it. I wanted to have a talk about the birds and the bees before the health class permission slip and before I stuck my hand down the front of some girl's panties.

I fell in love with books when I could admit to myself that my parents were not starring in *Father Knows Best* and I had to discover the answers for myself. I learned from the instructions in books and didn't have to wait for my parents to come around. In fairness, I should've been grateful for what I received from them, but I was too entitled, sitting in a five-hundred-year-old parlor slurping tea from a fragile china cup in Spain, to see beyond my own selfishness. All the driving from appointment to appointment with Dad, alone with my thoughts, was getting to me.

I had been driving for a good hour and a half. The two-lane road to Grazelima snaked along a narrow path with sheer drops on both sides beyond the road's miniscule shoulder.

I have never been a fan of heights, and the combination of a windy mountain road, a lack of guardrails, and not being sure where I was headed made me uneasy. It was morning, and a couple of cars had crept up behind me. I drove slowly. There was no place to pull over to let them pass.

They honked. I perspired.

After several miles of my not pulling over, which eventually became an act of spite from all the honking, they both eventually swerved around, leaving me alone for what would be the last twenty minutes of the trip.

I thought about what a crappy father I had inherited—a father who now sat beside me in the front seat in a black plastic container. I slowed to a crawl along the empty road and looked at Dad's remains. I said, "What a fucking jerk you are. Why am I here? Why didn't you get your new and better family to do this? Because they couldn't, that's why!" I waited, expecting some reply to diffuse my anger. Nothing came. No gentle breeze from a distant great beyond, only the sounds of the car's tires crunching along the gravelly road as I half expected to slide off of the mountain and to my doom.

"No really," I continued. "Where the fuck were you for the last fifteen years? And why the fuck did you not call?" The questions had been asked before, but it was the tone in my voice that was new. I slammed my hand down on the steering wheel until it hurt my wrist. I didn't even know why I was so angry. Dad and our estrangement was old news. For the moment, I thought it was the honking. Then I stopped the car completely on that empty road, my foot tight against the brake, and breathed in and pushed myself into the cloth of my driver's seat. I thought, *This should be easy. Dad is gone and there is no one to be angry with—except for maybe me.*

Maybe it was my fault for not trying harder to keep my relationship with him alive. Maybe all of my disappointment about him was not so cleverly hidden. He probably picked up on my feelings. Maybe I thought only about myself. Maybe life had overwhelmed him to the point that it became too painful to be with those who loved him the most. I expected him to have all the answers, but he didn't. Maybe it was my fault for not having more compassion for a man who handled problems by running away from them, for not knowing any better, because no one leaned over the open hood of a car with him and told him what to do. It was my fault for trying to be just like him.

If I still smoked, I would have lit up. If I still drank, I would have polished off every bottle I could get my hands on, including floor wax and a jar of maraschino cherries. It could have been poignant, perhaps even appropriate.

Fortunately, I had learned a couple of Dad's lessons well. I learned to give up. Or to give in. Or to surrender. I wanted everything to be easy. I wanted things to be simple. I wanted a simple relationship with my father.

My stepfather would have been much better at being a father. Ray came after Mom's fourth husband, Jim, died of a massive heart attack on her front lawn after injecting an eight-ball. She met Ray while still in mourning over Jim, when she had been volunteering at the Veteran's Administration teaching Vietnam vets how to play the guitar.

Ray is a straightforward guy who says, "I love you," and does not keep secrets. I am not sure he would be able to keep them, even if there were something he hid. Ray has a full head of silver hair and would often be described as fit. He had poor-quality tattoos with words like "Mom" and "Keep on Truckin'" on his forearms. Ray had a kindness to him. He also loved my mother and accepted her rashness without wavering or reservation. In many ways, he was much too good for Mom.

I told her so when they started dating.

He was a Vietnam vet who could help pull weeds from a tired garden or be equally valuable down a dark alley. Ray was likely the first man that would treat Mom well, a concept I think Mom was not ready to embrace.

Ray would have been an easy father to have, someone who had less that needed figuring out. Mom finally had a good guy who loved her, after the wreckage of my father's past, and Ray would always treat her well. I had a good stepfather, too.

I took my foot off the brake and rolled into Grazelima along the gravely road, and it was no longer anyone's fault, but nothing was forgiven. Not then.

***

AFTER A FEW MONTHS alone at Nothing's New and Dad officially living in Vegas, things began to get back to normal. I had adjusted to a new routine at the store. I was now buying, selling, delivering, refinishing, and appraising. However, I was not much of an entrepreneur. The inventory got low. Pockets where tables and chairs fit were now empty. What had been stacks of furniture three levels high was now only one. There were fewer glasses and bud vases. I had run out of African art after I refused to buy nine breakfronts that the African prince dumped in front of my store one morning. I had not shaved or taken a bath in a few days. My jeans smelled like beer and smoke. A couple of yellow Percocet rested in my pocket for any emergency, as well as a six-pack of beer in the tiny refrigerator by my feet. I sold stories well, but the risk of buying to make a profit intimidated me, so I avoided it. I learned everything I could about furniture, paintings, and collectibles. What I didn't know, I made up—it was now a second-generation tradition.

Before Dad moved, we had met up after a morning of walking the sprawling Rosebowl Swap Meet. When we sat in the truck, Dad reached in a bag and pulled out a framed pencil drawing of a clown holding the strings to a bouquet of colored balloons. The detailed drawing impressed me. Dad said, "It was done by a blind guy." I held the drawing closer to my face for inspection. Impossible, I thought. Dad laughed hard. "You dummy. Look at the thing." He took it from my hand. "It looks like a scientist made it with a ruler and protractor." Dad laughed again.

By the time Dad left, the story developed legs and each of us added new components to the blind painter story until he tried it out for real. He stood by the store's front window, wiped oil off of his hands, and pointed at the painting a young woman asked about. The painting was a portrait of a Viking captain and no one in particular. A painting that made me wonder why it was ever painted in the first place. I think it came with the store and was a total dud. Dad began, "The painter was a promising art student and noted for his use of highlights before he lost his sight in the war. It was really a shame." Over time, the "war" changed to suit the style and era of the painting. "After he lost his sight, he realized it was never the finished work but the process that inspired him. It was the feel of the brush in his hands against the canvas, the bitter smell of the oils, the stroke of his hand riding across the canvas. The actions inspired his imagination, inspired hope." Dad pulled over a stepladder and carefully pulled down the painting and held it like it was a priceless work of art, or nitroglycerin. Dad continued, "He realized he could still paint, draw, etch." The young woman leaned in for inspection. "But he wanted a goal. So he sought the help of art students, who outlined a little house on a hill. Or a tree next to a brook. Or the captain of the battalion, who treated him like a son.

"The students devised a system to set up a color palette. He learned to mix the colors by the weight of the paint on his brush. They stood next to him as he painted and guided him through a scene. And his love for the process of art eventually changed the world."

The young woman looked up at Dad, and as if on cue she asked, "Really, what do you mean?"

Dad ignored her question. "Scores of canvases, from artists all over the region, outlines of simple scenes arrived at his door. He painted night and day. He became so prolific they eventually trained a dog to help him paint when students were not available." Dad paused for drama. "Anytime he painted outside the lines, the dog would bark, which became the inspiration for the first seeing-eye dog."

While the woman stared at the painting with appreciation, Dad turned toward me and winked. After a few minutes of negotiation, she walked out of the store with a painting under her arm and an unbelievable story in her head. The game was so tasty, the story so touching, I almost believed it.

It was the perfect ruse for bad art and tripled the price of every crummy painting in the store. Thank god Wikipedia was still off in the future.

✳✳✳

DAD CALLED ME AT the store in the morning. It was before the age of caller ID and he enjoyed a newfound anonymity without my mother. I did not have his phone number, even though I asked him for it, but he called often enough that I did not worry about losing contact.

When the phone rang, I was sitting in the store at an old green desk chair that swiveled and was eating Oreos. The small table in front of me, which I used as a desk, was covered in unpaid bills and handwritten receipts, with a portable black-and-white television/radio that played daytime soap operas or jazz most days. I put down the bag of Oreos next to a large, billowing ashtray that smelled of ash and metal and sat on top of the bills.

"It's your father," Dad said. He had a way of announcing himself so his voice sounded like something that would grate cheese. I had grown accustomed to its sound. Since he had been gone, Dad and I had been getting along well enough, but I felt guilty for thinking poorly of him.

As I listened to his voice, I looked around the recently remodeled store. I had spent eight hundred dollars on the changes. It had brand-new carpet and a fresh coat of paint and it looked clean, but I began missing the morning flea markets and started sleeping in.

"What's up," I said. I picked up a glass that sat near my desk and began to polish it with a rag I pulled from my back pocket. The rag was a plant. I used it to get me out of the chair and show customers a busy worker bee. Look at that industrious young man. I started to look more and more like that crumpled rag.

Dad said, "Your old man has something to tell you. This thing isn't that important, but it is very *interesting*. Not sure how it's going to play out. You know, but it's hard to say for sure. But it is probably happening. I find it interesting, you might not…"

He yammered on in a vague way about some nondescript thing, prattling on between the heat in Vegas and something interesting. I knew that something was up, and I think he could have kept it up for another ten minutes if I had not interrupted.

"Okay, fire away, I am all ears. What's the mystery?"

From the other end of the receiver, I could hear him smack his lips and then take a long drag from one of his Salems. I waited for something big, important, or at least *interesting*. The sound of tobacco crackled in the phone.

Dad was a liar. If he had a secret, he wouldn't say anything about it or he would just make up bullshit without apology. But this seemed completely different. He spoke slowly. He paused oddly between sentences that were careful and measured. He lacked enthusiasm. His timing was off. There was something wrong. I put down the glass that I was polishing and went for my own pack of cigarettes and nonchalantly lit one, even though there was no one in the store to see my cool. I tried to wait him out, to see if he would break form and say too much, but the anxiety-producing quiet had won out, and I folded.

"Well!" I said.

He laughed in an uncomfortable way. "Not this time. Not this phone call. Don't worry. I'll tell you soon. It needs to be in person. But it's really interesting. Not good, not bad, just interesting." It was more yammering. He sounded like my aunt Rose, who sang songs that never finished but repeated the same two or three lyrics in Russian.

"Yes, interesting," he said, as if he forgot I was on the other end of the phone. He sounded distant, if not confused.

I said, "What the fuck kind of answer is that," trying to squeeze the information out of him with aggression. I squeezed the coiled phone cord in my hand until my knuckles whitened, as two thoughts that came to mind and left my mouth.

"Are you sick or something?" I asked. What I really meant to ask was, "Are you dying from lung cancer yet?" Something Dad seemed ripe for.

"Are you fucking kidding me?" he said. "I'll be kicking your ass when you're a hundred, and don't you forget that." I nodded, even though he was not in the room.

"Okay. So, are you getting married? You know, I would understand if you were. Did you meet someone?"

"Are you fucking out of your mind? I have a house with a Jacuzzi in the bedroom and a red Maserati and I am living in Vegas, flush with cash. What are you, a fucking jerk? I just got rid of your mother."

He did have a Maserati, a red *Chrysler* Maserati convertible. I had visited him in Las Vegas a few times after he had divorced Mom. He had a ridiculous house in a private, gated community in Vegas. Beyond the Jacuzzi in the bedroom, he also had an indoor swimming pool, and his living room was all mirrors—it was revolting.

However, his reasoning in that phone call made sense. Sadly, the news was not coming from a twenty-year-old friend about his bachelor lair, but from one of my parents. He was also in a relationship with Cathy, but I would not find this out for years.

"So you're dying right? I can handle it. Just tell me the truth."

"I did," he said. "I have some interesting information and I can only tell you in person."

"So what else could it be?"

"Calm down. What do you give a fuck about it anyway? But I will tell you this, it *is* very interesting."

And there it was. I had to wait and see him in person. As it was the middle of winter and I was the sole proprietor of a furniture store with no employees, I had to wait. I realized I was not breathing while I listened to Dad smoke. I tilted the receiver away from my mouth and let out a deliberate, quiet exhale. I did not want Dad to know none of this "interesting" business mattered too much, but it was all that I thought about for following months.

The same conversation repeated itself once a week for the next six months. We would try to talk about other things until he would eventually say, "So this news I have but can't tell you about is really getting interesting." I would press my ear tighter to the phone, hoping the shorter distance and extra concentration would yield a clue. I only heard the deep drags on a cigarette on the other end and smelled my own stale saliva that coated the mouthpiece of the phone. While he denied it, I convinced myself he was dying but joked about being his best man in the wedding he wasn't having. Inside, I waited for prickly news.

✳✳✳

DURING THE TIME DAD and I were communicating about that which was not to be communicated, I received a Federal Express envelope one morning with a single-paged letter giving me thirty days to vacate my store. It was signed by the Wooden Shoe Emporium, Ebba Andersson, the Swedish woman in the store next door; we shared a common wall and were friendly toward each other. She brought over cups of red Swedish glug, which was a hot mulled wine with spices, for the holidays. I helped her move boxes of clogs or sign for her UPS deliveries when she was not there. I read the page again and moved my lips as the words passed across my eyes. It was news to me that she had any right to evict me.

My store was a monster chore for few dollars. I had been making more money playing poker and bookmaking on the side with the help of a local coke dealer, but it was *my* store. To this day, I find it odd that she didn't just walk over, give me a sob story, and let me know I needed to move for one of four thousand reasons I might have bought.

I sat with the single page in my hand and read it again. I slumped back and my arms slid off the armrest. That fucking bitch, I thought. My mind raced across all the times we had sat and chatted with each other. We had spoken the day before. I picked up the phone to call Dad and put the phone down when I realized I did not have his number. I thought about locking the front door and leaving the furniture for someone else to throw away. Why did she need to be so distant and cold? I decided to confront her, indirectly. I paced around the store. I wanted to see where her head was at as I spilled some dark wood oil on a mahogany desk and wondered if I knew a junkie that would kill her. No one came to mind. I thought about a plan B, grabbed her letter, and marched next door.

Ebba sat in her usual spot next to the cash register in her empty little store. On one small wall hung a rack displaying wooden-soled clogs with brightly colored vinyl tops that had a thin layer of dust on each. *Did people wear these things?* I thought. I often wondered how she made any money.

I walked in with feigned panic. "Ebba, I just got this letter," I said, and I flashed it in front of her. I didn't wait for her to answer. "I think the bank wants *us* out, but I know we can fight this together. What do you say?"

Ebba crossed her arms across her ample chest and crouched, a move which made her look small. She got red in the neck and stared blankly over my left shoulder. She refused eye contact, even when I purposefully shifted my weight to the left and into her field of sight.

"It's not us, just you. Umm, I am, umm, evicting you." Her voice cracked at the end and when it did, I felt in a place that wanted to cry and punch her in the face at the same time, a helpless rage. I felt betrayed, but I was playing poker. I understood the rules of engagement, but I wasn't smooth at it. I felt my face get hot and my throat clench.

"But why didn't you just talk to me before this letter?" I asked, my own voice cracking at the end.

I do not remember what she said, but I remember how I answered. My response had been rehearsed before I walked over to her store. "I am so disappointed, but I understand. I promise to be out on the date in the letter. I know we will still be friends."

Ebba still couldn't bring herself to look at me. This small gesture might have saved a lot of future aggravation on both sides.

Nothing's New was being evicted by the evil Swedish clog saleswoman. At twenty-two, I decided to act as my own attorney and purposefully made life difficult for all. I filed legal motions and read law books and shook my fist at the heavens vowing I would eat her for lunch. When I told Dad about it, I could hear his venom boil as he said, "Do not be nice under any circumstance. Just kill her." For the moment I celebrated the anger with Dad before hanging my head from an overwhelming sense of failure—but I planned to fight.

I hired my favorite of Dad's cronies, because he represented the only crony I knew: Manny. He was still short and wide and lacked the sense of knowing right from wrong, which made most feel unsure about being alone with him. But he always had a loyalty to Dad and the lure of making a few bucks was enough to make him loyal to me too.

The job was simple. I gave him a Darth Vader mask and a ten-gallon cowboy hat to wear to stop traffic along La Brea Boulevard to help me attract as much attention and make as much money as possible before closing the store. I picked up Manny most every morning and dragged him to every sale and flea market possible. Some mornings were improvised. "There, man. What do you think?" Manny said as he leaned out the window. I stared at the dresser and turned around to look at the back of the van, which was empty. "I think it could fit. But can you carry it without dropping it? It's on a hill, too." I said. Two houses away, a tall chest of drawers sat on the lawn. Parked behind it was a moving van. The house was quiet since we pulled up a couple of minutes ago. I said, "I am not sure this is a great idea." I looked in the rearview mirror to see if a neighbor was watering the lawn or trimming the hedges. The block was quiet. "I am going to open the back and leave it open. I'll walk up and take it. You roll up," Manny said.

He hopped out of the passenger's side and ran around to the back of my van and open both sides. I watched him through the rearview mirror. He sniffed loudly, clearing the contents of his nose into his mouth, and then spat on the street before he took off for the dresser. I eased my foot off the brake and the van pulled forward slowly as Manny ran up the hill. At the dresser, he wrapped his arms around it and grunted it up. He was loud, and as he took a couple of steps down the hill, one of the dresser drawers began to slide out. Manny leaned back and jiggled the dresser, the drawer still out but not sliding out farther. I held my breath as Manny shuffled toward the van, which still rolled forward. I thought, *I could slam the accelerator and split,* but the dresser was almost at the back of the van. I heard one of the dresser feet scrape against the cement as Manny disappeared behind the side of the van. Manny came around the back of the van and heaved the dresser on its back with a crash. I looked up and around to see if there was anyone watching. Then Manny climbed in the back of the van and pulled the doors closed as I slowly pressed my foot on the accelerator pedal and drove away. My fear of buying disappeared and my dislike for the Wooden Shoe Emporium grew, because the store seemed less a chore.

Manny took it upon himself to cause the Wooden Shoe Emporium as much difficulty as possible. He sat in front of her store and loudly sang spontaneous opera that reverberated through the Darth Vader mask until she closed her front door. Once closed, he posted homemade signs that read, "Closed" or "Moved to Sweden."

On warm days, Ebba would leave the back door open. I would give Manny a cane and let him "fish for shoes" between the wrought-iron bars guarding her storage room. I paid Manny three dollars for a matching pair of shoes. However, a single shoe, unaccompanied by its mate, was worth seven dollars. I paid him a little bit more to dispose of the shoes in a local sewer.

Then I became a lawyer. I asked the court for more time. It pissed off the Wooden Shoe Emporium, for I had my store for another two months and delayed whatever plans Ebba had. The second trial was also continued to a third trial when the judge suggested I get a real lawyer, which I did. I found a lawyer I met at Tom Bergin's, which made a lot of sense at the time. The results were not surprising. I lost my store. The judge had described the testimony of my father, Manny, and myself as "dubious, yet crafty and wholly unbelievable."

In the end, I kept the store a full six months longer than the date the Wooden Shoe Emporium had wanted me out on. It was a small victory. The entire time, I kept Manny as my right hand.

***

As planned, Dad had come into town from Vegas and picked me up the morning after the trial—ready, finally, to reveal his interesting news. Dad was shaky and not his usual self. He fidgeted and wrung his hands as he made small talk, and I braced myself for the inevitable bad news. We went to Tom Bergin's, where I had become a regular in my own right, having earned my own green-and-white clover stapled to the ceiling.

As we sat down, Dad ordered two straight whiskeys and looked at me and said, "What are you going to have?" I knew he was working on levity, but there was something, well, *interesting* that he had to say, and I wanted to hear it.

He continued on about sports and the weather and other nonsense. I listening to his ramblings instead of the subject I had waited seven months to hear about. He avoided eye contact, preferring to gaze into the mirrored Jameson sign across from us. Whatever this thing was, it was more than just interesting. Dad's hand trembled as he raised the whiskey to his lips.

We went through a couple whiskeys each, his knee bouncing so violently the whole bar shook. I knew he was dying but gave it space. It would not have been a surprise. Dad was huge and gagged on four packs of cigarettes a day, which had prompted Mom to say at times, "What happened to the guy I married? He was the best-looking guy I had ever seen."

I knew how hard this was for Dad, but it had been months in coming. I could hear the chattering of regulars, but I don't remember seeing anyone else but Dad. It was as if there were a dome around us that created blackness beyond its scope.

He started, "You know how your mother and I got married?" I nodded.

"Well, before her there was Helen." Dad then began to weave a complicated story of his life with another woman I had never heard of before. He seemed shaken by an invisible force but continued through a stream of cigarette smoke and upended shot glasses. He rambled and referred to history, places and stories I had not heard of before. I sat in full attention, squinting and leaning on my arm.

Dad and Helen were married shotgun style. The wedding photos show a youthful couple. The groom, Dad, sported a black eye and looked drunk. Helen was seven months pregnant and likely drunk, as well. First a baby came and then another, John and Nancy. Then Dad left Helen. He didn't go into the specifics of why he left, or whether he had been given the boot by Helen. I eventually heard a number of conflicting stories by both sides of the family. From what I could piece together, Dad joined the army, and while he was away, Helen hooked up with Al, an abusive former-military sort that drove Nancy and John out of their home when they were teenagers. Years after, Nancy went searching for her real dad, conceivably a better dad than the one she had been given in Al. It took her three calls and thirty-five years to find him. The rest has been mired in history and vague memories. Either way, I now had a new brother and sister. When Dad finished talking he slunk in half, deflated and exhausted.

I shrugged. *Was that all?* I thought. *Was that the big deal? A life prior to me?*

On the plus side, I had been an only child and that was all about to change. Before I made the pronouncement of all being well, Dad's unsteady hand produced a photo of my brother, John. "He looks just like you," Dad said, handing it to me.

The shot was taken from fifty feet away in a light drizzle. He wore full subarctic attire: a bulky, hooded jacket pulled over his head, fingerless mittens, dark sunglasses, a scarf wrapped around his neck and mouth, and a full beard. John's pink nose was exposed. Everything else that could have been an exciting discovery of brotherly resemblance was left to mystery. The photo was also out of focus.

I took the photo in my hand and inspected it more closely before turning to look on the back to see if there was any more information, but it was totally blank.

I fanned myself with my brother's photo and said, "Are you sure you aren't just dying?" To break the tension I smiled. I liked the idea of having a new family somewhere in the Midwest. However, this obscure photo seemed a little too ridiculous to buy all at once. It seemed like a red-flagged prop.

"This one is a little vague. Do you have one of Nancy?"

"I am not sure," Dad said, pulling out a handful of photos. These would turn out to be school pictures of my new six nieces and nephews, but no picture of my sister.

I remained both excited and skeptical. We talked Dad sat up straighter, and he looked more at ease. "See, I told you it was interesting," Dad said. We parted on good terms, both drunk on a day of Jameson straight whiskey.

New Year's Day I found out for sure. The phone rang. It was still too early to wake up from all-night partying. Once the answering machine chimed on, an unfamiliar voice chirped, "Hey, Dev, it's your brother, John..." The slurred timbre of John's voice had to make him family.

Two days later, Mom invited me over, claiming she needed to talk to me about something. It was fine, considering I had some "interesting" news for her as well and needed to do a load of clothes in her washer and dryer. I went over in the morning, under the threat of her breakfast.

I grew up in a house where the "F word" was food. She had a knack for the experimental, a laissez-faire attitude that kept good recipes at bay.

In the kitchen, an exposed cube of butter sat resting on the counter that every feral cat in the neighborhood had licked with their germ-infested little tongues. That day, Mom made me a runny mushroom omelet with melted cheese.

"Thanks, Mom, you outdid yourself," I said as she entered the dining room with some cold toast and the cube of butter.

"I almost forgot your toast."

"That's all right," I said, and continued working on the omelet. "I'll pass."

"So, you can't stay long because I have art class. Do you remember when I told you about Susan? She was the tall lady wearing the wig. Remember, from the art show in the basement of the community center last year? You stopped by, under duress I might add, because you shouldn't give your mother any pleasure in life by just coming without me having to call you six times. Well, Susan just did this painting of some building in Italy. At least, I think it was Italy. Well, it was awful."

While Mom talked, Strudel, Mom's stray cat, hopped up on the table and began to clean itself two inches from the butter. Its tongue gathered bits of fur and debris into a small collection on its hind leg before it was distracted by Mom's diatribe and began looking around the room.

"Some people should just not paint. Speaking of that, have you seen my latest masterpiece?" Mom got up and returned holding a frame. On a three-foot-wide canvas were several splashes of muted colors, which I guessed to be a small house in a green jungle and an ominous, white-crested wave that happened by.

"Wow, this one is really good," I said, feigning interest. "So why am I here?"

"I know you. You barely even looked. I painted this in five minutes. Now you are going to say something very sarcastic," Mom said. "You should appreciate my art more, as I have one foot in the grave already."

"Okay, it is really very nice."

"Good. Thank you. Was that so difficult?" Mom said. "Did I tell you about my dead toe? Have you ever had a dead toe?" Before I answered, she said, "Did he tell you about the others?" It took a moment before I pieced together the change in direction of the conversation.

"Oh, do you mean John and Nancy? Yes, he told me about them," I said.

"Good," Mom said. "So, were you mad at him?"

I thought about this for a second in spite of the fact I had no bad feelings about the whole thing. "No," I said.

"Good. So he told you about the others, too?"

As it turned out, there was not just one other family but several, a gaggle of other potential siblings that Dad had created with women across the US and, as I later found out, possibly India.

"Are you sure you're not mad?" Mom asked. She walked out of the room with her painting before I could answer.

"I don't really know what I am right now. I guess I am not angry. It sounds like there's a bunch of brothers and sisters running around.

It's a little intense, but I can take it," I said. "Now, spill the beans. What do you know?"

She took a deep breath and slowly exhaled. "Don't tell your father I told you this." Then she sat down and started with the most recent. "Well, there was Phyllis Monroe." Mom said this with a long pause between the first and last name in a way that was riddled with sarcasm. Then she worked backward, deeper into history, until she brought up Helen, John, and Nancy.

In the beginning, Dad would not admit to anything beyond those who were actively looking for him, Nancy and John. However, there may have been as many as eight others.

"So how do you feel about all this now?" She waited patiently with her arms crossed. I looked skyward and considered how I felt. This all had nothing to do with me, but there was something not right about it either.

In the moment, I went with, "Good."

Mom then took another long, slow breath. "Okay, you never answered me about the toe. I think my toe is dead." Mom got up and walked out the front door and motioned for me to follow her. "Since today is honesty day." Mom began to shake. She took me to the garage. The garage was dirty and dank, with cobwebs hanging from the bare wood studs. Mom walked to a nonfunctioning refrigerator and pulled out an old box and set it on a table that was covered with paintbrushes.

She carefully opened the box and sifted through its contents before she pulled out an old black-and-white photo. It was a picture of Mom in a wedding dress, with a wedding cake and a completely different guy.

"Is that you and the guy who baked this cake?" I asked.

"No, that's John, my second husband," she said.

Mom and I talked while she shook through her confession. I tallied up all the weddings. Dad had a slim lead, seven to five.

***

THE LAST TIME I saw Manny it was three o'clock in the morning and I was coming to from a deep sleep. The pounding on my front door with a garbled version of my name put a lump in my throat. I started to climb out of bed. I lived on the corner of Packard and Fairfax, a fairly dubious corner at the time. The multi-unit building that I lived in had been painted a dayglow orange, but at night it hid behind several shady trees that attracted mosquitoes, crack dealers, and the occasional hooker. I became accustomed to the fights next to my bedroom window and the loud warbled voices wanting to know the availability of this or that, but never did they bother to come round to the front door to hassle me.

My girlfriend at the time, Chris, said, "What are you doing? Don't answer it." Oddly, had she not been there, I would have pulled the covers to my chin and waited until the pounding stopped. Instead, I felt I had something to prove by confronting what was on the other side of the door.

I sidled to the door holding the hatchet my father had kept on his dresser for protection. A pair of brass knuckles with a folding knife on the end sat next to it. Together they symbolized the passing of the torch of home protection from father to son, and I liked to pretend that I was a tough guy by owning illegal weaponry. My heart pulsed so hard I thought it would pop. When I got in front of the door, I heard Manny's voice laboring. This was only a little comforting.

"Devin, it's me, Manny. Open up." I looked through the eye in the door and saw Manny's distorted face and blond Afro as he continued to pound.

"Calm down," I said. "Are you with anybody?"

The pounding stopped. I could almost hear the gears sputtering in Manny's head.

"It's me, Manny. Open the fucking door already. Uh, yeah."

While I considered Manny an ally of sorts, he was still a drug addict, thug, and all-around criminal. There really isn't any honor among thieves, no matter what they say. I walked into the bedroom and told my girlfriend that it was okay, although I had my doubts. Then, I opened the door a crack.

As usual, Manny was sweating, slack-jawed, glaze-eyed, and out of breath. He pulled on his nose and then made a honking noise that was a combination of nasal and guttural, which led him to wretch and cough up some phlegm that he spat on my welcome mat.

"I have some really good news," Manny said, and walked straight into my apartment. I wiped the sleep from my eyes and closed the door behind him after looking out the door to see if there was anyone else waiting.

Once the door closed, I wondered why I had opened it in the first place. Manny was dangerous, and I really only liked him for the same reason I liked butterscotch and Barbra Streisand records: because Dad did.

"Okay, so what's up?" I waved him toward my tiny living room. I went into the kitchen, cracked open a beer, and brought Manny one too. Manny didn't say a word until I sat down next to him on my torn sofa bed.

Manny wiped his palms on his dirty jeans as he talked. "I need some money. Not a lot of money. But I have to have something done. A procedure. I need this thing done." Then he looked up at me and waited. I understood his ploy. He wanted to see where I was at. He was sizing me up. How much money could he get from me? Did I want to know about this procedure? He waited to see if I was going to give something away that he could use to make this process easier or more profitable. He studied me for a moment before he wiped his hands on his jeans again.

While I knew he carried a gun with him at all times, a small .22, and had a fat hand that he would think nothing of pounding me with, I stilled myself with long breaths to look confident and relaxed, exuding the image of someone not to be trifled with.

Someone who would not use the word "trifle" when negotiating with a crackhead, for instance.

"I can score some teeth—all of them. I can use some dental work." Manny leaned forward and opened his mouth wide, but he didn't need to show me. I knew that Manny had only a few teeth remaining in his head. He was a human Jack-o'-lantern, and his breath smelled like someone left a cantaloupe in a suitcase in the sun for a month before opening it.

"I need," he said, "I need one hundred twenty-two dollars. Yeah, I found this dentist who can put a whole set of permanent teeth, permanently in my mouth for one hundred twenty-two dollars. He's a student dentist. You know, the guy who goes to school. The guy says he can fix my other teeth too, yeah." Manny wiped his nose and sniffled deeply and wiped his hands on his jeans.

It was such an exact number. A number that would be hard to question, because it was meant to sound like a retail price for a dentist to charge. Of course, the number was also the most obvious flaw in his story.

Manny kept talking. I was still thinking about the brilliance of Manny's choice of number. One hundred twenty-two dollars was not going to cover even one tooth, let alone thirty-two new teeth embedded in his head and major surgery to fix the decay and rot from pounds of drugs that had passed through his soft tissue and released all his teeth from his mouth from the beginning.

Manny explained that these were discounted teeth, and he could get better teeth for another fifty-four dollars. Manny was not looking to get a big score from me, just a short-term fix, and one hundred twenty-two dollars was plenty for tonight.

I was sold, but I didn't want to take any chances. "Listen, I just went to the bank today and deposited all my cash, but I think I have the one hundred twenty-two dollars, unless you wanted to take a personal check?"

Manny smiled at the notion. A personal check would be worthless to him at three fifteen in the morning. While there was no honor among thieves, there was a code. We would play out this idiotic teeth-replacement charade. There would be no further conversation about the money or anything else, because the negotiation finished. I said, "Meet me around back. My girlfriend is sleeping."

There was no around back, but Manny knew to leave and I would be out in a minute.

I tightly folded $122 in cash in my palm and walked out into the street. I shook Manny's hand under a streetlamp. He held my hand for an extra moment and said, "I will get this back to you tomorrow morning. I promise." It was the code talking. He then pulled his hand away with the $122 and pushed it deep down into his pocket.

"No problem. Glad I could help," I said. Manny turned and began to walk down Fairfax Avenue. "I look forward to seeing your new smile," I called to him.

He turned around, looking confused. "Huh?" I waved him off and he continued on his way. It was the last time I saw him. Truthfully, he could have asked for a grand and I would have given it to him.

Chapter 6

A FEW DAYS LATER I got a frantic call from Daria while I was in Jerez. They had found a singer. As it turned out, the first mezzo-soprano of the Sevillian Opera House was in town for a benefit, and she knew "Ave Maria," and knew it well!

Daria said, "Yes, yes, she will do it. It would be very exciting. She happens to be in town. This would be fitting for your father, yes?" I pressed the flip phone to my ear for about a minute and listened to Daria's enthusiasm.

I was excited to know more of the charitable spirit of the fantastic lady soloist until I discovered that the one song would cost me six hundred euros. "Six hundred euros seems very reasonable," I said, but I almost threw up in my brain. I didn't blame her for wanting to be paid for her time, special consideration, and talent. I assumed her pricing structure also came from the likelihood that I sounded like a mental patient dragging around my dead father for a writing assignment. There was the reality of my pocketbook, at least that was the excuse I cooked up. I could have dug up the money if I decided to move forward with the mezzo-saprano. I just did not think Dad deserved it. Daria cajoled and I dreamed of the impact on Daria's psyche had I forked out the cash to see Dad serenaded off into the great beyond by a real pro, but I had already decided against it.

I took my time before answering Daria. I wanted it to look like I was considering the generous offer, discount pricing, and efforts toward making Dad's final launch a memorable one. Had I been in better spirits, thought better of Dad, had I been less self-centered, I would have, perhaps should have, jumped at the chance. It would have made a great story. I was just much too angry. I wanted him punished. I offered fifty bucks to any damn person who could sing that damn song—a song that I had not even heard before.

I went back to my hotel room, changed into a bathing suit, and jumped into the hotel pool. I told some sunbathing German blumkins that I was an Arabian Sheikh—it was more reflex than anything. Later, I propped Dad on the balcony for the sunset. I told him about the poolside girls and that he should have left me an inheritance. I also said, "So you know about the singer? Well. You know. It's all process. I am working on it. I'll forgive you eventually."

A few days later, I got another call from Daria. They found a willing student at the local conservatory of music who had a soft spot for my story. She was glad to come out for thirty-five euros. She was nineteen and promised to wear black. I quickly agreed and hung up the phone feeling a sense of accomplishment, like I had done him a huge favor. In reality I felt like I had gotten away with something.

I drove through the town of Jerez looking for a bodega, for an interview with the owner. I never found the place. Dad sat in the back seat after I asked directions for the winery and instead picked up a hitchhiker. After I told Dad the good news about "Ave Maria," I thought I heard cheery rustling coming from his black plastic home.

***

SHORTLY AFTER MANNY DISAPPEARED with a mouthful of impressive teeth, I had gotten word from one of my aunts that Dad "might" be holed up in Phoenix with his older sister, my aunt Alice. I had not seen or spoken to Alice in ten years, but I remembered how they talked to each other, sat closely, laughed at the same things, and how Dad found every opportunity to have his arm around her.

They were close. She and I were not.

Her number was faded but legible. Calling her made me nervous. I expected awkward small talk that led to my awkward transition to ask about Dad. It felt like the call was disingenuous, and it was. However, my life had been all about being nervous, awkward, and disingenuous.

It was before the digital age, so the phone rang like normal, but only with too much treble and an empty hollowness, as if I had called the abyss. As it rang, I decided no more than six rings and I would not leave a message, if it were an option. I wanted to keep my options of calling her again open without looking like a stalker.

On the fifth ring, she answered.

"Oh, hello," Aunt Alice said. While it had been years, I knew her voice well enough to recognize it. She had a gentle, Midwestern twang that swaggered with authority. It was similar to my father's. I imagined her wearing a bright red, short-sleeved sweater with a simple gold cross dangling below her neck.

I said, "Hi, Aunt Alice, it is me, Devin, from Los Angeles. George's son." No one called Dad George, his baptismal name, except his brothers and sisters. Like most everything, Dad hated it. I continued, "I thought I would touch base."

She said, "Oh, you would like to speak to George? I think you have a wrong number."

"No, no, I would like to speak to my aunt Alice. Aunt Alice?" I asked.

The silence lasted several seconds, almost to the point that dared me just to hang up before she started, "Oh, let me see if she is in." This was lame. I heard her breathing into the phone, waiting for time to elapse. Stupider still, she did not even try inventing a second person. There was no pretend conversation on the other end. No mumbled or hushed tones or pantomimed footsteps across a squeaky wooden floor, just her breathing into the phone.

Even though it was clear to me I was, in fact, already speaking to Alice, I was not surprised by her reaction. There had always been an unwritten law among Dad's siblings. While they might fight among themselves and not talk to each other for years at a time, they would never give up information to an outsider, anyone who was not part of their sibling clan. While I was Dad's son, I was not part of the initiated group and therefore not to be entirely trusted with even the most meager of information. For a moment, I wondered whether my aunt would go as far as to tell me she was on an extended vacation on a remote island and unavailable for months, before she spoke again, "Oh, Hi Devin. It's your aunt Alice. How are you? Is everybody okay?"

"Hi Aunt Alice. Everything is great." I told her about my family and my fascinating bout of unemployment. She told me about her kids and her grandkids. We talked about my other aunts and uncles and cousins galore, until the conversation began to organically sag as I paced around the room and its cold floor in my bare feet and waited to turn our discussion toward Dad's whereabouts.

Then Alice went with what I believed to be a preemptive strike. She asked, "Is your dad okay? I have not heard from him in years."

Well played, I thought.

"I know, Aunt Alice. I have not heard from him in years either." I exhaled more audibly, more frustrated than planned. "That's why I was calling. I certainly didn't want to bother him or anything, but I just wanted to pass along that I was thinking about him." Aunt Alice knew something and I didn't want to give her the opportunity to deny it by asking her directly.

Alice took several measured breaths into the receiver. "While I have not spoken to him in years, I have a friend that speaks to him sometimes. She said he was doing really well."

It was my turn to think and breathe into the receiver. "Friend" was such an odd word to associate with Dad. After Manny, I wasn't sure if Dad had any friends—even Manny stretched the meaning of friend in an oblong way. Dad had people that he had coffee with in the early dawn hours, but these people never had names or details attached to them. The more I thought about it, Dad was a loner.

I strangled the phone cord around my finger until it purpled while I debated whether or not to push the envelope. I wanted to pin Alice to the wall to force her to give me specific information. I also knew a direct confrontation over the phone would accomplish nothing, and then it stopped. All of the anxiety and interest finished. She had already given me something valuable. Dad was still alive and doing well, according to this mystery friend. My desire to know more just left, and so did the desire to track Dad down any further. I released the cord wrapped around my finger and the blood flowed back.

Alice and I chatted for another twenty minutes about nothing in particular. She told me about needing the garage door fixed. I told her about me getting a new-but-used car. Just before we ended our last call together she said, "You know, I love you."

I said, "I love you too."

After my call with Alice ended, I wondered that night why she did not just say, "Listen, Devin, your dad is laying low and does not want to be found," but mostly, I had a small epiphany. Phone calls like these had lost their charm and Dad didn't want me to know where he was. It was a painful realization. In the following days, I debated telling people Dad was dead.

Sure, I made a few more phone calls and participated in a few more rounds of hide-and-seek with relatives, but I had given up. I stopped looking for Dad. I told myself I no longer cared about him. This realization took place after speaking with Aunt Alice, or a few months later when I called Dad's brother, Fred, who assured me that he would have Dad call. Or when I spoke with Uncle Rick a few months after that, who was now a pit boss at the Peppermill in Reno, who told me that he had not spoken to Dad in months but would be sure to let me know if he showed up at the Peppermill. Or maybe it was when Aunt Jesse said...

It did not matter. Dad was hiding, and I became tired of cutting off my circulation by wrapping the phone cord around my fingers. I was in my mid-twenties and understood who Dad was because he had told me. He always said, whether he sat on a barstool or at Thanksgiving dinner, "Your old man is like the wind." It was a charming line. On the surface, it pointed to Dad's strength, and people smiled when they heard him say it because it had a folksy, almost pagan ring. I understood it to mean, even at a very young age, my father was unreliable and unpredictable. He was being exactly who he had always been, even though I wanted him to treat me differently than the rest of the world. I wanted to feel like I had a special place in his life. Hell, I was his son, after all. Now that I was less like an only child, I had more reason to see his wind-likeness. I felt betrayed.

Then it hit me: Dad's behavior was not about me. It was a brief moment of clarity, and I hung up the phone for good.

Dad cushioned himself from life for years, perhaps his entire adult life. The evidence was on display, and I had ignored it in spectacular fashion. I waffled between acceptance of Dad and a loud "good riddance." The thought of him drove me to bars and drunkenness. I pretended not to care, which manifested in more drinking. Now he cushioned himself from me. I leapt to the assumption that he must be dead rather than figure out my feelings. How else could he treat me like this? I went through a brief period that could only be described as self-inflicted mourning. I sulked and took handfuls of Vicodin that I kept in a Mickey Mouse Pez dispenser and felt sorry for myself for being an orphan. I ignored the fact that my mother was still alive.

All I knew was that Dad had left a paid-off building in Los Angeles and moved to Las Vegas with a red Chrysler Maserati that he drove with two feet, one on the brake, one on the gas—his love for action equaling his apparent love of smoking brake pads. He pissed the money away betting on the pass line and field rolls at the craps table and renting a mirrored house with an indoor swimming pool, and the cash dried up. The craps dealer's long wooden stick came and swept up all Dad's dough. He spent a relative fortune in a few years of looking strong and playing to impress. It had been enough money to keep him secure for the rest of his life.

In the meantime, I had moved just outside of San Francisco to a small town called Pacifica, to work on my drinking and penchant for dating broken women and feeling bad about myself. I took only what could fit in my trunk: an acoustic guitar, a small television, and a pile of clothes. I lived on the side of a hill that faced away from the picturesque Pacific Ocean and hung a heavy bag in the middle of the living room as I had developed a hobby of hitting things when drunk.

In the beginning, I took a sales job in the computer industry and worked as the one Caucasian in an all-Chinese company. I wore pressed suits. I showed up on time and rigged my phone by lodging a paper clip in the hock switch, then a string to the paper clip and the string to my wrist. I replaced my handset with a headset. When the phone rang, I raised my hand and was always the first person to answer sales calls. I stayed late and eventually convinced my employers that I deserved the title "King of Sales" on my business cards. At home, when I hit the heavy bag, I methodically placed a sponge across my knuckles, wrapped my hands, and taped everything to not injure myself. I put myself on a 4,500-calorie-a-day diet that consisted mostly of protein powder shakes and sweated myself into the best shape of my life.

My compulsive enthusiasm was short-lived. I began showing up late to work, stopped dressing in slacks, and started taking Valiums in the office toilet. Stopped making commission. A feng-shui master decided that I should have my office boarded up because of the money that was flying out of the door. When I got home, I lost the tape and wraps and pounded the heavy bag until my hands bled. My life was disintegrating quickly. The reason was only clear in hindsight.

I wanted to be the King of Sales, just like him. I wanted to be physically imposing like him, a drunk like him, distant like him, but I was disgusted by myself. I felt like I had succeeded in being my father and felt my world spinning around me, dragging me further down.

Dad called one morning out of the blue. I had not spoken to him in over two years. "Devin, it's your father." Although it had been ages, I acted casual and pretended things were better than they were with him and the rest of my life. It would be a common thread of presenting the opposite of the truth, no matter what. I had no money, so I quit my job, which made sense at the time. Then, I went to the local bar and bought the whole place a round of drinks. I had used Dad's advice. If you cannot be strong, look strong. Buying a roomful of acquaintances a beer insured I would get one in return and also made me look like a big shot to the drunken ladies at my local haunts. I was completely busted and waiting for my last paycheck.

"What's going on, chief?" I said.

"Hey there, sonny boy." He said it with song in his heart and a lilt of good humor in his voice. Without a pause and without a summary of the last couple of years, he said, "Float your father a deuce for a few days. I have something really big going on." Not even "how are you?" Then he let out a sort of chuckle that let me know all was good in the world. Floating Dad a deuce for a few days translated into me giving him two hundred dollars forever. He had floated me numerous pretend loans, although I was a teenager the last time I had asked him for anything.

Two hundred was not a lot of money under normal circumstances. However, my new normal searched all the pockets of my clothes for stray, crumpled dollars. I was sixty bucks overdrawn at the bank.

However, now was different, and I did not want to look as penniless as he was. "I would love to send it, but I have this thing going on over here, and most of my liquid is tied up. It's really wild, if I had more time, I would tell you about it."

Dad said, "I don't know if it is as good as what I have going on over here, but if you can't help out your old man, what's a caring father to do."

I reached for my cigarettes and found the pack empty. "How about in a few days? When I do I will send a tray." It was something about the way I said the word "tray," as if I were pushing my play by offering him more imaginary money. There was a waver in my voice. The kind of cracking voice that dogs understood as weakness. It spoke volumes to Dad. We both knew that I had no intention of sending him money. And hearing him take a slow drag on his cigarette from the other end of the receiver let me know that the game was up and I had lost.

The fact I had nothing to give him was irrelevant. I should have kept an emergency stash in case *he* needed it. I should have taken care of him the way he took care of me when he was around. None of these thoughts might have been a reasonable account, but it was the way we played. I imagined he would have robbed a bank, lied, cheated, and stolen to get me what I needed. During his long pause, I wondered why he was not lying, cheating, and stealing on his own behalf, but intuitively I knew he wanted the money from me.

His singsong voice flattened to disdain, a prerecorded message that played, "Yeah, that'll be great."

"Great, where are you staying these days, and I will get it out to you as soon as possible," I said.

He said, "Don't worry, I'll find you. Your old man is like the wind."

Then he hung up the phone, in many ways, for a final time.

I had avoided giving him two hundred dollars I did not have. I then shouted, "Fuck you, you asshole. Go find your own fucking money," at the phone that sat on the brown carpeting in my living room.

The guilt crept in. I should have borrowed money, sold my car, had a garage sale, and sold the heavy bag that dangled from the ceiling. Later that night, I knocked over an overstuffed amber glass ashtray into my brown shag carpeting and left the butts and ash in a pile on the floor. I punched the heavy bag bare-knuckled until the knuckles on my right hand tore open. The frayed skin on my hand seemed well-earned. When I finished punching, I poured alcohol over my hand and breathed in the pain.

On the plus side, the following morning I went and bought CDs on a credit card. I picked up music by Barbra Streisand and Garth Brooks and played love songs on my guitar while my heavy bag swayed from the ceiling. As much as I wanted to be some beer-guzzling tough guy, a charming, slippery character, I did not wear it well. I resented looking at the shoes people wore, looking for the outline of a knife in a back pocket or someone eyeing the crowd at the bar with too much interest. There were too many potential weapons and crazies. Living with Dad's paranoia was too much work, and the creepy dark cloud followed me everywhere. I was still trying to be like him and it had taken a toll. Without him, I preferred a good story. I was a straight guy that liked literature and show tunes. I needed a change but worried it might be in the genes.

***

"I WANT TO GO home." For her, this would be a medium-sized town in the Pacific Northwest. And she was my then girlfriend, Chris. We had been sitting on the couch in the middle of the night, neither one of us able to sleep.

She had silky golden hair, powder-blue eyes, full lips, and poreless skin that made her appear more honest than she was. She left block print notes that read, "Cee you thair in ten minuts," and then did not show up. She wrote many charming notes littered with spelling mistakes that became less charming as time wore on. Technically, she was my fiancée, and not my first.

I had come home in the middle of the night claiming to leave for a pack of cigarettes without returning and she met me in the street wearing an oversized blue nightshirt that had trouble containing her boobs. "You're an asshole," she said, and hit me across the arm.

I flinched, with my arms lamely defending myself. I wore a small T-shirt, which exposed my skinny arms to the night air, and extremely faded blue jeans with nothing but white strands at the knee that held the pants together. I stank of cigarettes and vodka, and I took several big steps back. Without thinking, I grabbed a handful of the strands and tore them out. When Chris moved forward, I took her hand and said, "I love you. I am so sorry." I twisted the strands and tied them around her ring finger on her left hand in a double knot. "Married in the eyes of God," I said.

I woke in the morning, my head filled with gravel, to Chris's voice on the phone with her mother. She sat on the green mohair couch I had taken from the store with her arm fully extended, admiring the twine wrapped around her finger.

Problem averted and another started.

I eventually found a hand-painted porcelain ring at a swap meet for five dollars when the "married in the eyes of God" ring disintegrated on her hand in a bar. Dad only said, "You're a fucking idiot, but she seems like an okay girl. Remember—this is it. It's not getting any better. So have an escape plan."

I didn't need one.

She said, "I miss the drizzly, gray days. It makes my skin prickle." Her reason was good enough for me. We looked for the fastest way to get her back home. That night, I surfed the alleys connected to several department stores until I came home with three cardboard television boxes and a thick roll of packing tape suitable for all her stuff.

I eventually put my then fiancée on a bus that left in the middle of the night from a bar that sold Russian beer and played quartet jazz to hipsters. The location was San Julian and Sixth Street, and we met the Green Tortoise bus line in the parking lot of the bar, a bus line known as being the cheapest possible means of transportation on earth and perhaps best known for caravanning Dead Heads around the country. The bus's doors vapor-locked open like Tupperware that belched out the smell of vacuum-packed garbage, body odor, and cheap dope.

Unfortunately, it was not Tupperware. It was a bus.

And it was not rotten eggs. It was people.

I looked at my future former fiancée with a bit of pity. As people rolled out of the bus to stretch and find oxygen, I held my breath and leaned into open doors of the bus to see what my future ex had to look forward to. There were worn sleeping bags strewn about next to boxes, tattered suitcases, and unconscious people. Everything was dusted in a distinct layer of cracker crumbs. The bus lacked seats, so people piled in on an open spot of awkward metal flooring to create what I saw as a human stew. It must have been even more disgusting once inside with the doors closed. I waved my girlfriend toward the entrance and said, "Seattle awaits," although I should have said, "This sucks. Let's get you a plane ticket," but I didn't. Chris hugged me one last time from the top step of the bus and climbed aboard before sitting down on an open bag of Doritos. There was no heart-wrenching final goodbye, and I watched the Green Tortoise pull away and cough its way through the vagrants and fog of late-night Los Angeles on to her new life without me.

In many ways, it paralleled my relationship with Dad, an empty, heartless goodbye. This was my bigger issue. What happened to Dad? Sure, I had grown used to a lifetime of his unreliability and even short-term disappearances, but this was different. It was the late eighties and Dad had officially disappeared. I was in my early twenties and had not heard from him in two years.

Little did she know, I had been told by Dad, numerous times over the years, that I knew nothing. I didn't know where he was living, where he was working, or how to track him down. It was easy not to know anything. I had no clue where he was. I was still moping around after Chris left but found pills, booze, and floozies a reasonable enough substitute, when the phone rang before dawn on a weekday.

I let it ring several times before answering without a hello—another tactic Dad taught me. A woman's voice began, "Hello. Hello.

Devin?" The voice wasn't familiar. She sounded upset and hurried. Between the time of the call and her tone, I knew it was likely about Dad. "Can I help you?" I asked.

"Is this Devin, Dave's son? He gave me your number," she said.

It would not be the last time Dad would use me as some sort of ethical collateral. Because I didn't know her and had been taught well, I repeated, "Can I help you?"

She was confused and out of breath. She said, "Yesterday, I locked up and there were forty cars on the lot. I told him, 'See you tomorrow, Dave.' And in the morning, nothing. Not one car. They are all gone."

As she spoke, I knew Dad had stolen all her cars.

"Who are you?"

She stopped talking for a moment, was taken aback by my question.

"I'm Sheryl," she started, making a point to fully articulate her name, "your dad's partner. I just don't know what to do. He always said not to call the police, but what if something is wrong?"

"Where are you calling from?"

Again, she stopped suddenly before slowly answering, "Our lot's in Florida..." She continued talking, but I stopped listening.

I thought, "Okay, Dad's by Fred, my uncle."

Fred was Dad's younger brother by a year, but the two could not be more opposite. Fred exercised and did not drink or smoke. Fred was reliable and stayed in the same place for his whole life. I made a mental note to call Fred later. As she talked, I felt little in the way of sympathy for her, but this call was good news. Dad was alive and doing well. He had just stolen forty cars, or its hot-market cash equivalent.

"I'm not sure what to do," she said, "so I called you. Do you know what's happened?"

She began to cry on the phone.

I told her I had to be at work.

Two days later, the phone rang again. She said, "I know you must know something. How could you not? He said you guys had a close relationship. He said you talked all the time. He's your father. You know where he is. If you don't, then you *should* know where he is."

She was right. I *should* have known where he was. I had been trained not to ask too many questions or expect too many answers. It was a futile place. She was angry. I knew the feeling well. When my sadness and disappointment did not stand up for themselves, my anger did.

I listened and paced around the room on tiptoes. The old hardwood had places it creaked. I didn't want her to think that anything she said held meaning for me. I didn't want to sound like something she said made me anxiously pace around a room on a telling floor. Still, her hostility made it easy to be a little passive-aggressive.

"Yeah, I don't know what to tell you, but I wish you good luck finding him, and tell Dad that I send my love." I detached, but with enough consciousness to measure in angry sarcasm, which I knew pissed her off. While her anger plotted to confront me, my indifference to her plight and loyalty to Dad had the same opportunity. Still, I didn't want her to get me involved in this, so I backed off. "Listen, I am sorry, I have not spoken to Dad in ages and I live three thousand miles away."

"What you did is illegal and wrong," she said, and then implied Dad was a shady character and that he and I had been planning this all along. Compassion crept in. I wondered what the woman on the other end of the phone looked like. That's when it struck me. I needed to end this call. I was not his caretaker.

I said, "Do you think he would make a big deal about my closeness with him, then have him give you my number and then when you get screwed, you think he is going to come to me telling me about it? Are you nuts? You lost your business. I lost my father. I'll probably never hear from him again. For all I know, he could be dead trying to sell or protect your cars." Then, I slammed the handset down on the receiver.

I doubted he was dead, he was too slippery, but I did pace the creaky floors as if I were right.

Over the next several weeks, I received a few garbled phone machine messages from the sad woman in Florida, which ranged from fuming to distraught to pleading. Each message reminded me that her financial life was ruined. She was in debt. I also had heard nothing from Dad. I was right. Dad didn't call for a long while.

I never called her back.

***

AFTER I CUT UP my suits and threw them over the ravine near my apartment, I ran from Northern California. I spent months bouncing around Europe. I drank beers, chain-smoked, and chased women who spoke with strange foreign accents who gave me food and shelter. I funded the rest with a pilfered credit card from my mother. Emotionally, I vacillated between thinking I was bulletproof and wearing a macramé sweater vest. Dad disappeared completely.

I returned to the safety net of Los Angeles with a plethora of escapade-like stories and a swaddling malaise of sadness over my life that seemed more fitting of a midlife crisis. I was twenty-seven and had no game plan. Within a week of my arrival, I dreamed that I needed to visit a local spiritual bookstore where books would fly off the shelves and change my life.

In the morning, I visited the now defunct Bodhi Tree bookstore on Melrose. Strolling down the aisles of homemade bookcases, among the smells of patchouli incense, flower petal tea, and tie-dyed shirts, I browsed in the used section for spiritual books. I carefully scanned as I read the spines for something out of the ordinary, something that might jump out at me. I looked for the "change your life in a meaningful way" section.

I just wanted to believe in something and was willing to do most anything. I visited pointy-topped churches and bowed at synagogues. I cleaned the mikveh, which is a disgusting job. I read the Qu'ran, the Tao Te Ching, and Zoroaster. Over time I found my niche.

I was back at the mystical bookstore and picked up a copy of *Magick Without Tears,* written by the dubious Aleister Crowley, a nineteenth- and twentieth-century occultist/screwball. The book entertained me as I flipped through its complicated wording about spiritual alchemy, but what I found most intriguing, stuck between a couple of pages, was a business card that had a funny symbol and a phone number. I set the business card on my nightstand and I took it as a sign. I looked at the card every day until I finished the book.

The following afternoon, I picked up the card and dialed the number. My hand shook while the phone rang several times. I hung up from nervous excitement. I walked into my closet and pulled the chain to turn on the light. Then I walked down the hall and into the kitchen and opened the refrigerator. I sat down. Then I stood up. Then I dialed the number again. A woman's recorded voice said, "Please leave a message."

I hung up the phone. *What does that mean? Is it code for something?* I asked myself. I walked into my closet, then into the kitchen. I ate a yogurt. I sat down and called the number again.

The recorded voice answered and beeped. "Hi," I said, "I am not sure I should be calling you but perhaps I should." I stood up and paced around the living room. "If you think I should be calling you because I have the right number, please call me back. Maybe we have a lot in common." I didn't know what I was referring to. I left my number but not my name and hung up the phone again. I sunk my head in my hands and thought, *What the hell was that?* I had watched way too many horror movies.

Two days later, I came home to a flashing red light on my answering machine. I ran across the room and hit the play button as I jumped in place. The woman's voice said, "I am not sure who you are, but maybe you should have called. You have our number."

It was another sign. I called back immediately, bouncing across the room. I did not know it at the time, but I celebrated feeling that someone was going to fix me. I felt something better than any drug I had ever taken: I felt hope.

"Yes, I think I should be calling you. I just think that. What should I do? There is something to do, right?" I enthusiastically yammered for another minute as if I'd found a sack of unguarded money. Two days later I received an address inviting me to what I assumed was an underground lair, an underground lair meeting on Wednesday at seven o'clock at night.

The street was dark and the house set behind a large shade tree. The blinds were closed and a crack of amber light slipped between the curtains and out into the street. Whispers sounded as I stepped up to the landing, which had a big globe at the doorway with a huge, sturdy oak door that felt like bricks when I knocked on it.

"Come in," a voice said.

I pushed against the big door, which dragged on the carpet and revealed a crowded room of fifteen people squeezed together. "Have a seat," a man in his forties said, who sat in front of them and wore a dark sweater and had a ponytail. He held a whiteboard covered in gibberish. The room smelled of dry-erase markers and oldness. The people were an eclectic mix of hippies, preppies, slobs, and intellectuals.

After I closed the door, I sat on the floor and listened. It was the tarot, but Hebrew numbers and correspondences to the planets, and loads of symbolism that floated way above my head. The conversation and questions were as dense as the oak front door, and I was mesmerized.

Six months later, I found myself in a smoky room filled with the heavy scent of incense, blindfolded and being asked to adhere to strict principles and take serious direction to explore who I was and what I wanted, in the most flowery of arcane language, or face the awful and unseen consequences provided by an elegant, yet humorless, universe that rang more like Christianity. It was the most fantastically creepy moment in my life, and I had no idea what I was doing.

I stood dressed in a white robe, which could only be described as an ill-fitting dress. After a multitude of wordy speeches from the guy with the ponytail and a few somber agreements on my part, I found myself initiated into the top-secret world of modern occultism, which is a little bit of witchie-poo accoutrements, unisex robes, and alphabet math.

Occultism, for me, was an escape through complex rituals of symbolism taken from the ancient Egyptians and Kabbalists. It called from the writings of Golden Dawn mystics that came from the late 1800s of Victorian England. I poured through their writings like I was on a mission. On the surface, and to the laymen, ceremonial magick is both comic fodder for horror movies and real-life evil that attempts to get chummy with guys that walk around on cloven hooves. Both views are not at all accurate.

On the inside, the cult, my cult, was structured with lots of homework that had much more to do with self-awareness than wickedness and reading a variety of sacred scripture. Actually, most of the initiates were just looking for a safe place to be who they were hoping to be. It was all so dull but manageable, and it encouraged change. I quit smoking, drinking, and drugs. I entered into long-term, although volatile, relationships with women who had zero interest in reclaiming their inner Raven or hearing the astral Moonsilver song.

This world was not as crunchy as it sounded. Rituals were to be performed in exactness in order to juice the symbolism in its most meaningful way and thereby creating the best-altered states of consciousness. I studied Hebrew, tarot, and the tree of life, whose glyph offered the most mental masturbation. It was fun, but thick and hard to digest, like a double bacon cheeseburger. I felt important and enlightened, though neither was true. I learned Egyptian mythology and wrapped the whole process into a flimsy notion called Thelema, which combined Eastern philosophy into Western mysticism. My brain billowed like sheets drying on the line on a windy day from all the possibility life and consciousness held.

I was still fairly new to the whole "secret society" thing. Without pills, cigarettes, and booze, the inside of my head became a flashing billboard sign of every wrong I had committed or felt was done to me. I found a hobby to get rid of some aggression and regrow my lungs from years of chain-smoking: running.

The museum was nearby, and I ran in a pair of old-school gray sweatpants, which had been cut off at the knee and had a drawstring. I wore a white bandana (so my grand Caucasian-ness would not be confused with either Bloods or Crips) on my head, schmata-style, and an ancient pair of white high-top basketball shoes. The soles had worn through, but I ran with them in the rain anyway. It had become a routine.

I ran around the tar pits and up the back entrance, past the harmonica-playing hobo who never missed a day, and around the hilly grounds. Over the course of a month, my initial trudge of jogging, I slowly learned how to run.

It had rained recently, and the streets were damp and uncrowded. One of those small, almost regular moments in life that made the tumblers click together into a lesson learned—as if by magic—soon followed. As I started to put on my high-tops, I found something inside the shoe that impeded my foot. When I shook out the contents, out rolled a severed rat head. It looked up with a half-snarled expression and its black marble eye stared at me. The sight barely fazed me.

Clearly it was a gift from the cat, a special present to me from her. As the rat keep staring at me, I noticed a little severed rat hand, with its little rat fingers about a foot away. About a foot from the rat sat a small pile of rat gizzards. I got a newspaper and scooped up all the bits of rat. After I cleaned up, I started to leave for my run, but then it hit me. Where was the rest of the rat?

I crawled on all fours with a flashlight looking for rat parts, under the bed and under a chest of drawers and all over the house, because it is not okay to have half a dead rat in my house. The thought stuck with me.

It was obvious. The pills, booze, and cigarettes were the rat I could see, but what about the rest of the rat? It was this thought that kept me on a quest of sorts, and one of the sole reasons I had to start looking inward.

Dad would have said, "What the fuck is going on with you? Don't shit me. Are you loony tunes?"

The old me thought my newfound spiritual self was an idiot. I was both proud and ashamed of it. I was the morality pendulum swinging as far away from my father as possible, but I didn't know it at the time.

I marched along on a new road and every couple of years Dad would show up at the front door, haggard and unshaved. His breath progressively labored and smelled like a sewer. And he was distant, like when he had stayed switched off the last time he asked for dough.

He arrived as if we were friends that had drifted apart. His hugs were not as tight or powerful, but maybe it was his age. Dad was aging rapidly, in his late fifties/early sixties. His beard was gray but his hair still chocolate brown, though thinned and waved lifeless. His teeth had fallen out and were replaced by awful dentures that filled his head with bright white, ridiculous-looking, jumbo chicklets. His body was still bloated but not as strong. He shrank. He lost the spunk and swagger that I idolized. He took breaks walking up stairs from exhaustion and still smoked cigarettes like they were a cure rather than a cause. Rumors swirled from Dad's family that they were tired of giving him money.

Over the next several years, I thought about Dad and whether he had been on the run and hiding because it was too hard to look for the rest of the rat. The only thing I knew was that whatever he was doing, I needed to do the opposite.

Over the next ten years, I saw Dad just a few times. Each time he was smaller. Each time he had less to say. Less fire. Each time I pressed a couple hundred in his hand before he left and then I felt like shit. Each time he took the money the same way a homeless guy on the corner did, but without saying "God Bless you" first.

Each time he left, I closed the door behind him in a way that I thought it would be the last time I would see him, secretly hoping it would be, but he kept coming back.

My life had turned around and I was in search for half a dead rat. While I still thought of Dad often, I mostly lost all respect for him and all the emotion I had for him. I saw him and felt almost nothing. I also cut him no slack for not living up to my expectations, for not aging with dashing style like Lyle Waggoner or Tom Selleck. He was a blob that he had just given up on life. We headed in opposite directions. He slid to a logical destiny, and down the path of justifiable anger and self-righteousness. It took me another decade to realize that I was a self-important douchebag.

Chapter 7

I RETURNED TO CÁDIZ midmorning with two hotel appointments left for the afternoon. I was tired and needed to wipe the sweat on my brow on my sleeve often. Maria stood in the lobby of her quaint hotel with one of her employees, holding a handful of brochures. She wore a thin summer dress and a yard of eye-popping Mediterranean cleavage. She spoke almost no English, and she was perfect. I was a sad guy preparing for his father's seaside funeral. She spoke Spanish the same way warm butterscotch tastes. Over the next forty-five minutes, I asked her to marry me. Eight times. My stupidity requiring her employee to awkwardly translate.

After making an ass of myself at my previous appointment, I got in my rental car and left Old Town Cádiz. The car was empty as I drove to a modern hotel in the new part of Cádiz and banished Dad to the car's trunk because I had enough. Dad was slipping away.

New Cádiz had high-rises and even fresh cement walkways that skateboarders love, and wide streets without shadows from all of the efficient street lighting.

I arrived to find code-height curbs and brand-name coffee places on every corner. It was all so generic and familiar. The hotel sat by the ocean, but I couldn't smell the saltwater or fresh bread in the air. The streets lacked the bustle of people and little shops. Cars whizzed by, making the only movement around me a blur. I left what I imagined Dad would have loved about Old Cádiz and the rest of Andalucia.

I could see why Dad would have loved old Cádiz, even if he had never visited. The city had character that creaked in the wind but was far from used up. Its vibrancy and charm were unmistakable. As I drove away from old Cádiz, I left his old world behind in exchange for a bland one, a fucking orderly, ordinary, corporate world. The new section of Cádiz had conveniences but lacked adventure and the spirit of the unexpected. The realization filled me with melancholy. Everything was clean and sanitary, and predictable. I sat in my rental car and felt alone.

No one was riding shotgun with me anymore, and soon Dad would officially belong to Spain. My feeling about Dad's new reality and my life without him seemed permanent but fragile. I was now sentenced to live out the rest of my life as a sober, corporate dud.

I had one final meeting that day. I met with several business guys all named Pablo, who represented a five-star hotel chain I would stay at in Nuevo Cádiz. They all wore double-breasted dark gray suits and starched-white button-down shirts, and all parted their slicked-back hair on the left side. I wore the same green linen shirt I had worn all day. It was crumpled from my suitcase and smelled of overripe armpits. We met on the fourth floor in a high-tech office with glass walls and a long oval table that overlooked the hotel's pool. I realized the Pablos were everywhere and the people who were not Pablos aspired to be them, and I wished I had a gun so I could kill myself.

The Pablos offered me rehearsed small talk and corporate jargon about luxury business centers with breakout rooms and expensive dining and Internet options at a premium. I should have been writing it all down for a future story about business travel in Spain. I didn't pretend to care. I didn't pretend to take notes. I kept my hands behind my back, clasped together, as they walked me around the hotel's presidential suite or poolside or through the impressive spa that smelled of sandalwood incense. They were polite, and I wanted to smash them all in their identical faces.

Instead, I smiled vacuously, nodded at appropriate times, and occasionally said things like, "uh huh." As they took turns talking about their hotel's amenities, I pondered being half an orphan and began to understand luxury as being synonymous with triteness.

After my hotel tour, I numbly thanked the Pablos for their kindness and expressed my insincere desire to work with them in the future. I gave them all firm handshakes and left with an armful of hotel brochures with glossy covers featuring airbrushed white women wearing wide, floppy hats next to pools of glistening water. Along with the brochures, there were neatly packaged DVDs of the hotels with press releases printed on customized stationery with raised letterhead.

When I got to my room, I waved my credit card magnet key in front of my door and it magically unlocked itself. I threw all the brochures, DVDs, and press releases in the wicker garbage basket in the corner of my free room, courtesy of the Pablos. I threw Dad on the nightstand then flopped myself on a bed of one-thousand-thread-count sheets and played with my credit card–sized room key.

My mind drifted to Old Town Cádiz. I thought about how Old Town Cádiz's hotel keys were the old skeleton kind that had giant brass fobs that took up too much space in my pocket and offered little security to my room. They are the keys of gamblers, I thought. Houdini could never decipher modern locks, making his tricks useless in a modern world. Those clunky skeleton keys with tarnished brass fobs had seen better days and had lost their value in a modern world.

Dad would not have seen it that way. Dad would have said, "Those fucking keys are our history. Everything in life is supposed to be imperfect and inconvenient and a bunch of fucking aggravation. Then once in a while you have an adventure. Then you get to tell a story, and that's your history." Actually, Dad would have said, "It's your fucking history, jackass," and punctuated it with a hand gesture that pantomimed hammering a nail. It would have made sense to me, and maybe only me.

I fell asleep in my pants and woke with small Spanish coins that fell out of my pockets during the night and stuck to my belly in the morning. They left an imprint. I threw Dad in the trunk along with my suitcase for the homestretch for our return to Old Cádiz. While I grew fond of toting Dad around in my backpack and carrying on conversations with shadows, I knew it was going to be an emotional day. I was going to a funeral and needed some space.

After a couple of tourism meetings in the morning, I returned to Old Cádiz on Friday around two o'clock in the afternoon. The city felt strained, like remaining coffee grounds trapped in a filter. The shops looked hollow, cats napped uncomfortably, worn pedestrians shuffled along, and I felt it all in the back of my throat. Cádiz had somehow changed, but not completely. All those tiny cars pressed up against each other, in rows along the road, a claustrophobic's parking nightmare.

And so began the merry-go-round experience of finding a parking space in Cádiz. Parking anywhere in Spain is a hassle, but I learned over my two-week visit to park accordingly, just like everyone else. I parked on the cobblestoned sidewalks, on the exposed roots of giant elderly trees, on the patio of a restaurant, and once I double-parked on a one-way road, trapping miles of passengers behind me while I visited the dingiest bathroom of all time.

I drove in increasingly larger concentric circles around unusually shaped blocks, getting farther and farther away from my destination. This was fine by me. I was not looking forward to saying goodbye to Dad or my newfound friends at the tourism board. They took all my confusion, bad Spanish, and additional requests on Dad's behalf in stride. I looked forward to their occasional check-in calls, but I was not feeling grateful.

I eventually found a nice spot several blocks away from Cádiz Tourism under a big shady tree, and I left Dad to meditate in the car. The weight and the reality of scattering my father's ashes finally took form. It was awkward and cumbersome, like trying to carry an empty refrigerator box. My arms could not reach all the way around it, and I could not know what was ahead of me, but I moved forward with faith that there would be solid ground with every blind step. Faith has never been my strength.

I began to sweat. I cleared my throat like I was sick. I felt light-headed. I took a deep breath and smelled the warm bread of a bakery down the road, the sea air of Cádiz, and the exhaust of too many little cars. Everything I saw had a bluish haze to it.

I took the tiny elevator up to the fourth floor and felt my cheeks flush and the bile in the back of my throat build. This was it. This was the funeral that my father never had. It wasn't the jovial celebration that I'd hoped. When the door to the elevator opened, I walked in expectant. Where was my singer? Who should I talk to first? Should I sit or stand? Be patient or not? I had a switch in thinking. I hoped that the girl from the conservatory arrived early so we could just leave and get this thing over with. I did not want too much time to loiter around the office. I tried to look up and make eye contact, but I didn't want to see anything. My vocalist was not anywhere.

It was 2:30 p.m. and I wandered and listened to the office buzz. People walked back and forth, speaking quickly on the phone. I imagined my return to Cádiz to move smoothly with a light tone, maybe some joking with Daria and Cesar, but I just wanted this done. I wanted to see a young girl dressed in black with big boobs and a Viking skullcap with horns preparing for an aria. The image felt important as a beginning, an ending, and a symbol of completing Dad's final wish. Daria waved and smiled from her desk and said from across the room, "I'm sure she is just running late." I wanted to walk over to her but felt glued to the patch of carpet on the perimeter of all the desks.

I stared at the clock on the wall, watching the second hand slowly grind around in a circle. After two long minutes, I turned around to see if anyone was coming out of the elevator door. I walked over to Cesar and tried to act casual. I had taken a liking to him during my brief stay the first time around in Cádiz. Standing there with my hands in my pockets, I rocked back on my heels before I spoke.

"So, any word on the singer yet?" My breath was short and anxious.

He looked up from his game of Windows solitaire, smiled, and shook his head. "Nada, but don't worry," he said. "She will come."

But she didn't come, which left me to pace. I finally walked over to the corner, where Daria was sitting. Then to Juanita, who simply shrugged her shoulders at me.

Over the next forty-five minutes, I continued regular combinations of pacing, clock watching, and panic. And still no sign of a songbird. I know the office rooted for me, which I found reassuring considering I must have been becoming a pest.

Finally, at 3:15 p.m., Daria received the call. I raced over to her desk along with several others who were now pacing along with me. After several long pauses of Daria nodding her head with melancholy, she told me, "Your young singer from the conservatory said that, regrettably, she will not be able to make it. She has come down with—" Daria then bent down and began to fish around for something. She pulled out a Spanish/English language dictionary and pointed to the word, "laryngitis."

While in time I would to come to appreciate the beauty of the situation, at the moment, I began to crumble. Without needing to say another word, the entire room stopped and snapped into action. They picked up their phones to make calls on my behalf. I should have been grateful, but I was too self-absorbed to see much beyond my immediate need. I could only wonder how a room full of Spanish people could not know how to sing "Ave Maria"? Isn't it the Catholic national anthem? However, I had never heard the song either, because my father, a Catholic, didn't want me to know anything about the religion. He told me one too many stories about having chalkboard pointers broken over his head, scolding and smiting nuns peddling dogma that he wanted nothing to do with. I was helpless and returned to helpless pacing and quietly prayed that my new Spanish family would come up with something.

The minutes stretched by. Friday afternoon in Spain was the wrong time to get anything accomplished. I felt my time in Cádiz slipping away. A couple of other ladies approached me just to smile and be nice. But I didn't want their attention, I wanted a solution. I didn't want to feel alone and vulnerable. I wanted to give Dad the exact send-off he wanted and look tall and confident doing it. If I did, maybe success would undo forty years of a failed, despondent relationship. I could feel like I was a good son. But it was not meant to be.

Daria approached me, looked at the ground, and said, "I don't think we can help you."

My throat tightened, and I prepared to run into the street screaming for help.

Then I heard a sound from the back of the room. It was coming from Cesar's computer. The sound became "Ave Maria." It was beautiful. The classical woman's voice became the catalyst for all the emotion and denial that I had been holding on to until that very moment. I felt the tears rolling down my cheeks. I couldn't breathe and then I did what any other self-respecting pseudo-alpha male would do: I ran to the nearest door and closed myself behind it. I would've kept running if I had not walked directly into an office supply closet. The only thing that I could see was a brief crack of light at the bottom of the door.

I stood alone in the closet for several minutes until there was a knock on the door. Before a feeling of stupidity settled, the door slowly pulled open and the light poured in. The kind of light that let me see all the small specks of dust twist in the air and the kind of light that turned a beautiful woman's skirt transparent. Daria flooded in with that light. She was the most beautiful woman I had ever seen, backlit by what I now reminisce as a somber light.

In that moment I understood God.

She handed me a triangular paper cup of cool water. She tried to look me in the eye but instead looked to the ground and took a deep breath. "We have decided that you will not do this on your own. We will come with you, to hug you and kiss you. We will hold your hand, and we will mourn with you. You are safe," and she stepped out backward, never raising her eyes to mine, and closed the door in front of her. When she left, the light left with her. It was here that I realized I missed my dad and never wanted to say goodbye. I sat alone, surrounded by reams of paper and paper clips, toner cartridges, and the dull ache of unwanted transformation.

When I walked out of the closet, the small office looked meaningless with the fluorescent lighting lowered and the Tourism Office of Cádiz waiting patiently for me, to close the office for the week.

I cleared my throat several times, trying to find the words, but none came.

Everyone was ready to leave, with coats and briefcases in hand, when Daria came up to me and said, "Cesar found 'Ave Maria' on the Internet by one of the most famous vocalists in all of Sevilla and made a CD of this song for you." She exhaled loudly and then smiled broadly. "We will all drive together and find the best spot in all of Cádiz. Anywhere you want. And then we are going to play 'Ave Maria' for your father. And together we will mourn."

Four people I did not know waited for me outside while I walked on uneven sidewalk to get Dad one last time. My throat was still tight, and I felt a light breeze against my damp face. For a brief moment, and for the first time since I arrived in Spain, I felt gratitude and perhaps some relief. I smelled cinnamon by the bakery and sea salt in the air. I passed uncomfortable cats and worn pedestrians. I inhaled a small dose of peace, which came from being right in the middle of the moment, one foot in front of the other over loose cobblestone.

"Dad," I said to myself, "I think you chose well."

I walked in acceptance through my father's adopted home until I came upon the big shady tree. At its base sat nothing. I stared at the empty spot before looking around trying to get my bearings. Many things crossed my mind, but the obvious was that Dad could not resist one cosmic final joyride.

My tiny blue car had been stolen, along with my dead father in its trunk.

I stood in front of the spot where I had parked my car, trying to make sense of the emptiness. I walked a block ahead and behind to see if it had rolled somewhere all by itself. Nothing. I walked into the space and walked back out and scratched my head. I put my hands on my hips, clueless, and stared at my feet.

I understood that the car was gone because, well, it was no longer there. There was action to take, but I could not think of what that entailed. My arms weighed heavy at my sides. My stomach and chest hollowed. I looked around to see if someone would come forward with an answer. No one came. I took aimless steps in every direction until I turned in a complete circle; my head swung back and forth to catch a glimpse of anything that would make sense. Several moments passed, and then I turned around and stumbled back to Cádiz Tourism.

My flight was leaving at seven o'clock from Sevilla the following morning. No car, little money, and no Dad. My knees buckled on the cobblestone from the heaviness of confusion. Up to that point in my life, I had attempted to believe in an organized, magical world that cared for its participants—or at least those who believed in said magical world. I hoped for a god that watched out for me, although

I never quite bought into the idea. I hobbled along as perspiration slowly dripped down my sides from my armpits.

On the plus side, I had a place to stay in Cádiz, but no idea how to get home from, or to, Seville. There were four people who waited in front of the tourism board. When I got there, I planned to lie down on the street and throw myself at their mercy as a pathetic, helpless blotch on the pavement. That's all I had.

I felt nauseated, and my head felt like it was made of balloon. The thought of leaving Dad unscattered and my relationship with him symbolically unresolved gave me a sense of dread. I thought I could barf out enough sadness for my tourism friends' sympathy, as if pity would drive them to wave magic wands and reappear Dad. It was an odd sense, as life was great. I traveled Spain for free. People were sympathetic and helpful. None of this made sense then, just the fear of losing my father and knowing how stupid I was for not schlepping him up the stairs to the tourism board with me. I passed the smells of warm bread on wobbly knees and saw my four familiar strangers chatting in a small circle.

As I approached, Cesar called toward me after seeing me empty-handed, "Did you forget your keys in the office?"

I did not answer, and the group waited patiently until I got closer. As I stopped in front of them, I said, "My car is not there." I know that I spoke the words, but no one was home.

I found myself sitting in the back seat of a tiny European car with Cesar driving, Anna in the front seat, Javier and Daria in back with me. Daria was sitting on my lap, but considering my state, this could have been wishful thinking. I heard the car's tires strain across the crooked streets of Old Town Cádiz. It was Friday, at the end of a work week, and I had lost Dad.

Yes, I knew I was a jackass.

Daria broke the noise in my head and tire sounds outside of it, saying, "You know, you are not the first person to have their car stolen in Cádiz."

Without thinking, I responded, "You mean with their dead father in the trunk?" Although I did not get the joke at first, the car erupted with laughter. The sound took me out of the hopeless future my self-loathing painted in my head, but I quickly returned to the present. I stared out of the window and looked closely at every small blue car we drove by. Everyone else loosened up. Anna began to talk in Spanish with pauses, which were followed by nods of agreement and more conversation among the four.

Anna then turned around from the front seat. "We are trying to figure out where to look for your car. It cannot be so far away, unless someone planned to put it on the ferry to Africa."

My whole body itched, but there was nowhere to scratch. The marble continued to roll around in my hollow skull. I then began to realize that all my sweating had an effect. My BO wafted in my face and it stunk. I forgot about Dad to think about how Daria wouldn't find me attractive, as if all my stupidity and crying were some big turn-on for her. Anna continued, remembering that I was still a journalist in assignment, "Cádiz is very safe, but things happen in every city. We also think that maybe you saw a red triangle on the ground where your car was parked. This means it was towed."

Towed? I thought. *That would be good.*

She slowed down and waited for my answer. She said, "The red triangle would be obvious."

I closed my eyes and tried to picture a red triangle in the space under the tree. I stopped thinking about my increasingly awful BO. *What is a red triangle?* I thought. I then realized Daria was sitting on my bladder and started worrying about urinating on her. If not for my stupidity, crying, body odor, and that I might pee on her, she could be mine.

Anna continued, "Well, we should start at a police station." We meandered around Cádiz until Cesar pulled the car over to the side of the road and Anna hopped out. She looked at me and said, "I will be right back. Wait here."

I sat in the car and heard my father's voice in my head, "Some jackass you are. You just left me in the fucking car?" I could still hear him take a frustrated drag from one of his Salem regulars. "Why didn't you just dump me in the water when you got here?" It had been ten years since I quit, but I wanted a cigarette. It was the prop I had used to punctuate any moment.

On the day I quit, I choked down eighteen delicious American Spirits cigarettes in a row, on the tile floor of my bathroom in my underpants. I threw all the butts into the toilet. Smokes were the tool that I had used to convince myself I was of age, a man. Mostly, I smoked when having feelings I wanted to avoid. After my final drag of the devil nicotine on that day in the bathroom, I flushed the toilet six times before all the butts would go down—like they never wanted to leave.

I stared out the window, hungry for nicotine, and watched my blue car not coast by. Javier and Cesar casually chatted in Spanish and laughed a few times as Anna appeared in the car's open window. She asked me, "What was the license plate of your car?"

I had no idea.

She asked, "Do you know the make and model?"

I had no idea.

Even if the police had towed the car, we needed to know which car it was and how to identify it. I drove that stupid car for a week and knew nothing about it.

"Do you know the color?" I did. It was blue. "Blue," she said, waiting for me to offer some more information.

Then I felt a gurgle in my stomach that started at my solar plexus, quickly descended into my colon, and ominously rattled down. The gurgle was unmistakable. My body was responding to all the stress with a gas bubble and about a gallon of nervous water that had just emptied itself into my large intestine. My face grew hot. Daria started to weigh a ton. If I had not turned her off by all the crying, body odor, stupidity, and potential urine, shitting in my pants would do the trick.

As I clenched, Anna started back toward the station, when she turned around. "Do you have the keys to the car?" I had them on the plastic keychain that was imprinted into my sweaty palm. I looked down and saw a small miracle. The keychain contained the VIN number, license plate, make, and model of the car. It was a small victory. Then I placed my arm across Daria's leg for a moment, until things felt too awkward and unfamiliar and I felt like a fool, and then I clenched tighter.

Anna turned around and disappeared. Javier, who had said nothing up to that point, began to speak Spanish, but I knew what he was saying while he gestured with his hands, "Of course, it was a rental car."

We could have called the rental car guy to get the information sooner.

A few minutes later, Anna returned to the car, her hair disheveled. "Good news. They have your car. But it is not here. It is…" Then she began to speak more Spanish. "We must hurry. It is Friday and the city department closes early for the weekend." Anna jumped back into the car and off we went. She turned to me and said, "We need one hundred six euros. You will have to pay for the ticket and the towing."

I had about seventy euros on me.

After what seemed like an eternity of winding streets and increasing traffic, we pulled over again. Anna turned to me and said, "Come with me." Daria lifted off of me, and I realized my legs were asleep. I limped down the block clenching, into the underground garage that smelled like burning oil and desperation, or maybe that was me, which was lit by a handful of fluorescent tubes that showed how the soot covered everything.

We walked around the lot until we found the dim glow of the glass cashier's cage. A tall man in an official-looking uniform was flipping through a large stack of pink papers. He had jaundiced coloring and his face drooped from years of disinterest and shuffling pink papers in a glass box in a photon-free zone.

We stood for a few seconds before Anna cleared her throat, waiting to be acknowledged. Nothing. After a few moments more, she launched a few decibels louder and said, "*Hola,*" which was followed by a lot of fast Spanish. He never looked up. She began to read off the car's keychain. He did not look up, but slowly turned, as if practicing tai chi, and pulled a clipboard of yellow papers. He licked his thumb and slowly waded through them. He spoke calmly and sounded a lot like the tires that churned over the cobblestones.

I did not understand a word.

She looked at him and then me. "We need more money."

I told her I did not have more money. I looked at the disinterested man behind the glass. I said, *"Por favor..."* but my crumbs of Spanish blew away in the underground breeze. I looked at Anna and shook my head. I pulled out my small wad of crumpled euros, giving her the coins as well. Anna exhaled deeply and banged her fist at the glass, holding my money. The disinterested man looked up after the second series of bangs. Anna's voice was soft and earnest, and I could feel her imploring the disinterested man to take kindly upon this weary traveler. She pointed at me, explaining my predicament. I looked down to my shoes, attempting to elicit sympathy.

The disinterested man shrugged his shoulders and went back to shuffling papers.

I took a deep breath and I held it until I felt lightheaded and let out a bursting gasp for air. Anna did not give up. She pounded the glass one more time, this time not waiting for the disinterested man to look up and started yelling at him. She pointed at me and said something that included the word *"muerto."*

Ah yes, *"Muerto,"* I jumped in. *"Mi padre es muerto en la bolsa en mi trunko de autobilio,"* I said.

The disinterested man looked up. Anna continued yelling in Spanish and kept yelling as she rummaged in her purse before pulling out her business card and pressing it against the glass. She pushed the card through the metal tray, the space that bridged the gap between us and the disinterested man. He did not take the card. She then turned to me and said, "Give me all your money."

I handed her the ten-euro note I had folded in the secret pocket of my jeans for an emergency and added all the money to the metal tray.

The disinterested man did not look up. He said, *"Un momento,"* and just stood there not taking the money or Anna's business card. This went on under the dim lights of the garage, the smell of oil making me sick.

Anna began tapping her foot. I wanted a toilet break desperately. The disinterested man flipped through some papers, saying, *"Un momento. Un momento..."* before he finally said okay.

Okay! I thought. *Please let this not be some odd Spanish word, meaning "fuck off."*

The disinterested man reached for a pegboard filled with keys in a tai chi maneuver I would later describe as "beyond the setting sun."

Even if the car were there, I had no idea if Dad was still in the trunk, or if I would find a toilet in time. I bounced in place.

Anna looked at me and smiled. After another ten minutes, the disinterested man, Anna, and I walked five feet to my little blue car, which I didn't recognize at all in the underground lighting. Anna handed me the keys and fumbled with them to open the trunk. I dropped them on the floor and then dropped them twice more while trying to pick them up. Finally, I got the key into the lock and popped the trunk. There was Dad, in the blue backpack next to my suitcase.

"Oh, there you are."

And I picked him up and slung the backpack with him in it across my chest. Anna and I jumped in my car and we pulled out from the parking garage, leaving the smell of oil and my desperation behind me, and, thank god, I found a bathroom.

We drove in tandem, Cesar leading the way with Anna and Javier, and Daria and me driving in my little blue car, in silence, along the crowded seaside streets of Old Town Cádiz looking for a place to say goodbye.

The crew from Cádiz Tourism had taken my absurdity in stride and with good humor. Now I sat alone with Daria, but I was caught between the exhaustion of having tracked Dad down and the burden of having to gather myself up to say goodbye to him. I felt drained, anxious, and, somehow, vindicated. Dad would have the send-off he wanted, with a couple of minor adjustments, and I could feel like a good son, perhaps for the first time in years. Still I lacked the energy and the words, Spanish or otherwise, to express any of this to Daria. There I sat, with this beautiful woman, and felt completely alone.

After about fifteen minutes of winding streets, Cesar pulled onto the curb after I found a scenic spot. Actually, I do not remember finding anything. I think they just decided to pull over after we had been driving around long enough. It was a good spot, though. Or as good as any. Charming, old world, teaming with strolling Spaniards on a cloudless spring afternoon. The location was on a street that jutted out over the sea, which made for an uncomplicated sending off.

Dad would have liked Cádiz, the soft breezes, an easy vibe that dropped my shoulders from my ears. As I unbuckled my seatbelt, I heard him say, "Represent your father well."

I got out of the car and walked straight to the cement railing about fifteen feet above the water that overlooked the Sea of Gibraltar and a distant African coastline. Everything seemed to move so slowly.

I sat my backpack on the floor and carefully pulled its zippers apart. As I did, I realized I had never opened up the black bucket before, not even out of curiosity. Not knowing what was inside sent a chill of nervous expectation through me. Would it be some sandy rubble and then a tooth or a piece of Dad's nose? My knees were unsteady to support my weight. I considered that all the things that Dad was would not be in the drum: his humor, charm, guile, and belligerence, not to mention his fatness, would not be there. At best, what I saw could only be the symbolic remnants that Dad was most completely, most certainly, dead.

I looked around and consciously took long, slow breaths in through my nose and out of my mouth. Daria, out of respect, looked down and shuffled her feet. Javier and Anna quietly chatted, and Cesar sat in his car and waited for his music cue.

For a moment, I was afraid Dad's whole head would be just squished into the bucket and would have to be pulled out by his hair. I pulled out the tub, let the backpack fall to the floor, and set Dad on the concrete railing, which overlooked calm waters that made a lapping sound on the shore below. I took a deep breath of salty mist and tried to slowly exhale in an attempt to control my emotions.

It did not work.

I heaved out a breath that staggered several times at the end. I slid my long thumbnail in the gap between the lid and the bucket's sidewall. I could feel the paper and plastic dig between the nail and thumb, cutting into me as I slipped along the two sides that had been taped down by a big white label that had Dad's name on it: Henry David Galaudet.

The top came off without any of the expected sound effects. No vacuum-packed belch or pressure hiss like when opening a can of minestrone. Inside was a sealed clear plastic bag that had a piece of white tape that held the bag closed, almost like what might be on the end of a cheap loaf of bread. I pulled the gathered plastic, like a handle, out of the black plastic jug. It was a snug fit, and I pulled hard to get the bag unmarried from the jug. I set the jug and lid on the floor and listened to the wind while I held the bag tightly. Anna and Daria stepped forward next to me while I readied myself.

I turned to Cesar and nodded. Then I turned back to the sea and looked out. The music started and filled the gaps of silence left by the wind and the rolling waves, and, for a moment, Dad and I were the only two people in the world. All of my anxiety and insanity cooled. So did my anger toward him. My legs felt secure under me. I was left with nothing but sadness. Not the hyperventilating kind that needed a paper bag, just a deep sense of overwhelming loss.

I punched open the top of the bag with my car key and tore it open wider with my fingers. That got gray ash on my finger, which I intuitively put in my mouth. It tasted like nothing in particular, and the act felt appropriate. I now know that if I were ever left alone in a room with moon rocks, I would eat them.

"Ave Maria" flowed from Cesar's car. It is a song made for sadness and mourning. I cleared my throat and heard my voice escape in short, weak bursts as the melody transported me back to a time when I was small and helpless but resilient. The breeze swept a light trickle of dust from the bag into the air. I resisted the urge to take a fistful in my bare hand and let it slowly pour back into the bag. I knew this was the time and this was the place to let go. It was finally finished, and I could say Dad was home. If there is an afterlife, I think Dad would have agreed.

"Ave Maria" kept playing.

I pulled out a printed email from Cathy. She had asked me to read what she had written. She started with "My Beloved" and wrote plainly of her sadness, gratitude, and their life together. It was short and apropos. As I put her letter away, I wished her well in a small prayer. Praying was something I rarely did when not feeling trapped in a foxhole.

When it was my turn. I pulled out my letter to him. The paper was frayed on the side from being yanked out of a spiral-bound notebook, and creased from being sat on in my back pocket all day. After unfolding it, I read the opening lines to myself. It was filled with hostile questions, finger-pointing, self-importance, and loads of judgment.

Intellectually, I knew that Dad had been dead for more than two years, so it did not matter what I said. Spiritually, I knew this was the last time I would do anything for him ever again. Was this how I wanted it to end? I wondered whether my questions and sarcasm accomplished anything. I wondered whether my act of service and love for him would be tarnished by an act of unforgiving defiance at the finale. I looked over at Anna, who dabbed her eyes with a Kleenex. She did not know about my history with Dad. She was at my dad's funeral and there to support someone she barely knew. I folded the letter up and put it in my back pocket. Then I spoke.

"Dad," I said. "I mean, hey, Dad. What's it like there? I just want you to know that I am grateful to have had you in my life. I know you did the best you could. I know that you would have been dangerous if you had been given a few more chances, like the ones you gave me. I wish I had been a more understanding son. I wish I would have held on to that broken BMW a little longer. I wish I had thrown you a few more bucks when you needed it. I wish I would not have changed the locks when you left the last time I saw you. I really feel bad about that one. I wish I had given you more credit for being the most important person in the formation of my life."

I took a long sad breath while Cesar restarted the song.

"Anyway, I hope to run into you when it's my turn to go toward the Light."

With that, I had nothing more to say. There was only one thing left to do.

However, on that day in Spain, surrounded by kind strangers who mourned alongside me on a pier in Dad's new home of Cádiz, a place that perfectly accepted Dad's imperfections as a father and a man, I poured him into the sea. Whether he drifted in calm waters to dissolve, be eaten by fish, settle at the bottom of the sea floor, or perhaps sail a benevolent current to northern Africa— it didn't matter.

He returned home, where his hatchet, brass elephant, and other human frailties were forgiven.

I leaned over the railing and watched him fall, like sand at the beach, between my fingers, the same way heaping cups of sugar naturally mix into a tall pitcher of lemonade on a hot summer day.

"A fucking lemonade reference? What kind of shit is that?" I heard Dad's voice call to me from a dark, smoky bar in the sky.

Lemonade or not, I think Dad would have loved Old Cádiz, with its warm smells and winding, imperfect roads that accepted him just as he was. When it's my time, maybe someone who is pissed with me will return me to a spot that looked out to Africa and set me adrift in my dad's home and find peace.

A long, thin, gray funnel of my father disappeared into the sea, to become some other thing on some other side. He will most definitely be kicking my ass when I am one hundred.

Author's Notes

I WILL FOREVER SEE my father through the eyes of a seven year-old. It means he will always be a little godlike to me. When I think of him, which is often, he brings forth a sense of wonder, mystery, and magic. He will forever be the toughest, most interesting, and most fascinating person I have had the pleasure to know. No one could take me so high or drop me so low. I don't temper my experience of him in these pages.

My memories are by their very nature imperfect. I can only acknowledge this flaw. I did everything I could, during the seven years I spent writing my story, to recreate scenes as I remembered them. I did the best I could to capture the nuances of our relationship and how I understood him as a father and a man.

I must also acknowledge Dad was a storyteller. I write about what he told me, and others, with a certain amount of question marks floating in the air—particularly around why he wanted to go to Spain in the first place. And much like my truth in these pages, I believe that Dad's stories were his truth.

I accept that family, friends, and even strangers might disagree with my take on all of this. It's okay. I can hope that they understand this homage contains my truth that must start and end with me. While I take responsibility and stand behind every word in this book, it was never my intention to hurt anyone, especially the memory of my father who continues to be my greatest hero, and to remember him only with a sense of wonder, mystery, and magic.

Acknowledgements

To ME, THIS BOOK is a miracle. Not because it is like the Bible but because I have no idea how *10,000 Mile with My Father's Ashes* got finished. Fortunately, I was not alone in the process. If it weren't for the consistent support of smart, talented writers who met in my living every Thursday night at seven thirty for our writers' group, none of this would have happened. Each week they challenged me, listened to my complaints, and encouraged me through rough drafts and final edits alike. Tisha Richle, Lisa Holdren, Kat Kambes, Lalanii Grant, and others showed up week after week with their own writing and snacks to share and make my week. They kept me accountable to my story and didn't allow me to settle for anything other than my best effort.

Once the story was finished more people offered needed criticism and feedback, responded to flustered emails, and encouraged me more than they could ever possibly understand. Krista Vernoff, Kent Black, Toni Ann Johnson, Ken Shapiro, and Seth Fischer, thank you.

Of course, the tourism board of Spain and Cádiz, who unwittingly helped write this book and took everything I did in stride with great hospitality. As a side note, I am proud to have written a number of articles about Spain and Cádiz. A place I love!

My publisher at Rare Bird Books let me sit in his office and ramble on about vintage guitars for two hours. Their fantastic support team, who also let me yammer on, are rock stars! For their support, encouragement, and the predestined way our partnership unfolded, I am grateful for team Rare Bird including: Tyson Cornell,

Guy Intoci, Julia Callahan, Hailie Johnson, and Jake Levens, who took a chance on this writer.

My mom, whose patience and endless zaniness have always made life fun, and made life with Dad seem marginally normal. Yes, I have always been an insolent child, and I appreciate all you had to put up with from Dad and me. Love always.

And finally, my wife, who I embrace as the perfect person to travel through life with. I have never heard her say with a certain exasperation in her voice, "I married a writer. Ugh."

I am grateful for all of your selflessness and good will. You will forever be my heroes.